William Charles Edmund Newbolt

The gospel of experience

Or the witness of human life to the truth of revelation

William Charles Edmund Newbolt

The gospel of experience
Or the witness of human life to the truth of revelation

ISBN/EAN: 9783741192692

Manufactured in Europe, USA, Canada, Australia, Japa

Cover: Foto ©Lupo / pixelio.de

Manufactured and distributed by brebook publishing software (www.brebook.com)

William Charles Edmund Newbolt

The gospel of experience

THE GOSPEL OF EXPERIENCE

WORKS BY THE SAME AUTHOR.

Crown 8vo. 5s.
COUNSELS OF FAITH AND PRACTICE.

Crown 8vo. 7s. 6d.
SPECULUM SACERDOTUM; or, The Divine Model of the Priestly Life.

Crown 8vo. 2s. 6d.
PENITENCE AND PEACE. Being Addresses on the 51st and 23rd Psalms.

Crown 8vo. 2s. 6d.
THE FRUIT OF THE SPIRIT. Being Ten Addresses bearing on the Spiritual Life.

Small 8vo. 1s. 6d.
THE MAN OF GOD. Being Six Addresses delivered during Lent 1886, at the Primary Ordination of the Right Rev. the Lord Alwyne Compton, D.D., Bishop of Ely.

Crown 8vo. 2s. 6d.
THE PRAYER BOOK: Its Voice and Teaching. Being Spiritual Addresses bearing on the Book of Common Prayer.

LONGMANS, GREEN, & CO.
LONDON, NEW YORK, AND BOMBAY.

The Gospel of Experience

OR

*THE WITNESS OF HUMAN LIFE TO
THE TRUTH OF REVELATION*

BEING

THE BOYLE LECTURES FOR 1895

BY THE REV.

W. C. E. NEWBOLT, M.A.

CANON AND CHANCELLOR OF ST. PAUL'S CATHEDRAL
SELECT PREACHER BEFORE THE UNIVERSITY OF OXFORD, 1894-5
AND EXAMINING CHAPLAIN TO THE LORD BISHOP OF ELY

"Existimabam ut cognoscerem hoc : labor est ante me donec intrem in sanctuarium Dei et intelligam"

LONGMANS, GREEN, & CO.
LONDON, NEW YORK, AND BOMBAY
1896

All rights reserved

TO

THE REVERED MEMORY

OF

WILLIAM JOHN BUTLER,

LATE DEAN OF LINCOLN,

TO WHOSE DEVOTED LIFE HIS OLD CURATES LOOKED

AS A

PRACTICAL EXAMPLE OF CHRISTIAN FAITH,

THESE LECTURES ARE DEDICATED

WITH ALL AFFECTION

AND RESPECT.

PREFACE

THESE lectures were delivered in obedience to an expressed wish of the Lord Bishop of London, which I did not feel at liberty to refuse. They labour under these two defects: first, that they were undertaken at a very short notice, when it was not possible to give them the amount of study which lectures of this character seem to demand; and secondly, that they are an essay in a branch of homiletics to which the author has not been naturally nor officially drawn hitherto.

The underlying idea which they try to develop is this: that just as the spade of the excavator is a valuable ally to the student who investigates historical records, so the spade of experimental inquiry, in the region of the spiritual life, ought to yield valuable confirmation of those facts which Holy Scripture leads us to suppose exist in our own lives, and in the constitution of things around us. And that just as the excavator concentrates his chief attention on places and scenes where ancient life reached its fullest development, so our inquiry will, in all probability, be most fruitful if, instead of spending time in investigating the actions of the average man, we in each case interrogate the highest forms of spiritual development within our reach.

I wish to express my grateful thanks to the Rev. J. Storrs, for allowing me to deliver these lectures in the Church of

St. Peter, Eaton Square; and to kind friends who, in various ways, have helped me in preparing them for publication; while I earnestly hope, that if they seem to contribute but little to the solid strength of apologetic theology, they may at least indicate a region which lies open to scientific investigation, in the lives and conversation of those who rightly or wrongly protest, "We have heard Him ourselves, and know that this is indeed the Christ, the Saviour of the world."

W. C. E. NEWBOLT.

3, AMEN COURT, E.C.,
Mid-Lent, 1896.

SYNOPSIS

LECTURE I.

THE SENSE OF A PERSONAL GOD.

                                                                             PAGE

I. Introduction 1–4

    Practical rather than scientific atheism the prevailing tone in the seventeenth century, when these lectures were founded. Practical atheism, and agnosticism, and a form of Deism, the most prevalent form of unbelief at the present day. An endeavour made to rescue revelation from the charge of—

        effeteness 5
        and inutility . . . . *ib.*

And to show—

        its practical importance 6
        its bearing on common life 7

Hence the choice of subject 8, 9

Explanation of method—

        not on a wide historical scale 10
        but by interrogating individual experience . . 11–13

On such subjects as—

        the existence of God . . . . *ib.*
        the Fall . . . . *ib.*
        Sin . . . . *ib.*
        the punishment of Sin . . . . *ib.*

	PAGE
Grace	13
Not again generalized experience	14
nor on the low average level	ib.
but Christian life in its highest development	ib.

II. The subject of the present lecture 14, 15
   The testimony of human experience to the general assumption of revelation, that there is a personal God . . . . ib.
   1. This seen in the phenomenon of reverence for an unseen Power common to religions 16–18
      carried to its perfection in the *rationale* of worship in the spiritually developed man . . . . . ib.
   2. In the phenomenon of the sense of guilt common to religions 18–20
      carried to its perfection in the consciousness of the spiritual man, who has the sense of an offended judge, and of a moral arbiter of his actions . . ib.
   3. In the phenomenon of prayer common to religions 20–23
      Reaching its fullest development in the spiritual man, who walks with God, and is conscious of a Divine Presence 21–23

III. Objection to the subjectivity of the method, briefly considered 24, 25

LECTURE II.

THE TRACES OF A FALL—WITHIN.

I. The origin of evil an ancient puzzle 26, 27
   To which, however, Holy Scripture professes to give the clue in the narrative of Genesis . . . . . ib.

	PAGE
Objections to this narrative from—	
The consequences which seem to flow from Evolution	28–31
The higher conception of human nature	31
The character of the narrative in Genesis	31–33
Real difficulties of the Fall	33
The method to be pursued in this lecture	34, 35
the interrogation of experience	35

II. The constitution of man, exhibits *generally*—
1. A mixture of greatness and strange depravity . . 35–38
    the overshadowing of melancholy 37
2. Particularly
    a complex arrangement into three divisions— . 38–40
        Spirit 38
        Soul . . . . *ib.*
        Body 39
    But strangely warped by being subject to—
        natural degeneration 41–43
        great disorder 43–46
        capacity for degradation 46, 47
III. These witness to a catastrophe like the Fall . . . 48–50
    which was not the starting-point of Progress, but of
    human depravity and confusion . . . . . . *ib.*

LECTURE III.

THE TRACES OF A FALL—WITHOUT.

This is to be seen in the infinite disorder of the world . 51
I. The environment in which men live—Is it helpful or the
    reverse? 52

Testimony of Revelation. St. Paul describes the creation as subject to failure 53
This statement examined 54–56
Practical importance of the inquiry 57
II. Man at his highest development is conscious in his spiritual nature of an adverse power called *the World* 57–60
The intellectual faculties of man are disturbed by false ideals liable to lead him astray 60–69
The physical man is confronted by pain 69–71
How pain is met by Christianity . . . . *ib.*
III. True progress, what it means, and to what extent it is possible 72, 73

LECTURE IV.

THE PHENOMENA OF SIN.

These only to be adequately accounted for by the Scripture record 74, 75
I. Pervading character of these phenomena in Holy Scripture 75–78
The *differentia* of sin as such 77
II. These phenomena equally pervade ordinary human experience 78
As may be seen—
from the phenomena of religion 78–80
in the testimony of representative writers . . . 80–82
in the testimony of human language 82
III. The most characteristic appreciation of sin discovered in the lives of spiritual men 83–85

SYNOPSIS. XV

	PAGE
The reason of this discussed	85
Expressed as follows:	
1. In the sense of failure to reach an ideal	85–89
2. The sense of injury to a person	89–91
3. The sense of impotence in the presence of an adverse power	91, 92
IV. Hence sin is regarded, both by revelation and experience, as	92
a mistake	93
a catastrophe	ib.
a loss	94
and must be treated with all seriousness	94–97

LECTURE V.

THE PHENOMENA OF TEMPTATION.

Human experience bears direct testimony in this to the Divine record	98
I. Holy Scripture persistent in its witness to the presence and working of an adverse power of evil	99
This no allegorizing sentiment	100
no impersonation of subjective feeling	ib.
Holy Scripture precise as to the existence of a personal Tempter	101
The growth of this testimony	ib.
The testimony of our Blessed Lord	101–104
II. Does experience corroborate this testimony?	104
1. The ancient oracles and ancient mythology	ib.
Possessions	ib.
Devil worship, ancient and modern	105

		PAGE
Spiritualism, etc.	. . . .	105
The common phenomena of temptation	. . . .	106

2. The testimony of a spiritual man will confirm this, and exhibit the phenomena in the most acute form . . . 107
Importance of believing in an evil person, rather than in a principle of evil 108
The strange fact that the good are attacked as well as, or more than, the careless 109
The strong malignity of attacks 110

III. This experience bears testimony to the distinct characteristics of the evil power, which are crystallized in his titles 111
   1. Devil 112–117
   2. Satan 117, 118
   3. Murderer 119
A spiritual man the best judge of spiritual phenomena 119, 120

LECTURE VI.

THE PHENOMENA OF THE PUNISHMENT OF SIN.

I. 1. The revelation of the punishment following on sin, as giving us an insight into the character of sin in itself 121–124

2. The difficulties of the statements of Revelation as to future punishment examined 124
       Universalism 125, 126
       Restitution 125
       Conditional immortality 126
All explanations agreeing in this, that the statements of Holy Scripture are most severe on the subject . *ib.*

SYNOPSIS. xvii

	PAGE
3. The Atonement in its bearing on the subject	126, 127
II. Experience presents equal difficulties	127
1. Is the punishment of sin here, what antecedently might have been expected?	128
2. Is it "just"?	129
3. Is it "merciful"?	130, 131
III. The characteristics of the punishment on sin, which we see around us, bear resemblance to the punishment denounced on sin in Revelation	132
1. Permanence	132–136
2. Severity	136–139
3. Loss	139–143
IV. Recapitulation	143, 144
The worst punishment of all	144

LECTURE VII.

THE PHENOMENA OF REDEMPTION.

I. A strain of Redemption to be traced in Revelation	145–147
This redemption using the world as it is, and acting in spite of it	146
1. In the form of a promise, developing hope	147
2. In the developing of the sense of moral obligation under the Law	148
3. In the Incarnation	148, 149
II. So in human experience, we trace—	
1. The development of character, in, and out of, and in spite of, environment, which yet always remains "the World"	150–154
2. The longing for a higher ideal, the wish to be good running through different stages of life	154–159

3. The power to be good, produced by strengthening the will	159–166
4. The achievement of goodness. Christianity presents the highest type of character in the world	166–170

LECTURE VIII.

THE PHENOMENA OF THE ATONEMENT AND GRACE.

This, the gathering up of the Redemptive strain of Revelation

I. Examination of the testimony of Revelation on these points . . . 171
   1. *The Atonement.*
The eternal purpose	172
Early sacrifices	ib.
Levitical sacrifice	ib.
The Cross	173

There must be no shrinking from the Scripture doctrine thus summed up—
"A full, perfect, and sufficient sacrifice, oblation, and satisfaction, for the sins of the whole world" 174–176

2. *Grace* 176
Prayer	176–179
The subjective benefit of sacrifice	ib.
The gospel scheme of grace	ib.

The two-fold purposes of atonement and sanctification illustrated by the parable of "the Good Samaritan" . . 179–181

II. The confirmation of experience 181
   1. Alleged neglect of the doctrine of the Atonement, and reason for it 182

Tentative endeavour to find traces of the Atonement—

    in the world 183

    in individual experience 184-186

2. *Grace.*

    In its bearing on heredity and environment . . . 186

    Importance of the question 187

    Heredity dealt with by Holy Baptism . . . 188-190

    environment by—

        Absolution 190, 191

        Confirmation . . . . *ib.*

        Holy Communion 191

    Short recapitulation 192

LECTURE I.

THE SENSE OF A PERSONAL GOD.

I.

" He hath set the world in their heart."—Eccles. iii. 11.[1]

WHEN Robert Boyle, at the end of his life in the year 1691, left provisions in his will for the foundation of a course of lectures, "expressly against Atheists, Deists, Libertines, Jews, etc., without descending to any other controversy whatever," he spoke out of a life, passed in a period of storm and stress which has never been equalled in this country.

He had lived to see the Church and State both

---

[1] This passage may be understood to mean, "God hath put eternity in men's hearts," *i.e.* the faculty of considering and being moved by the past and the future; or, "God hath framed the mind of man as a mirror or glass"—"capable of the image of the universal world, and joyful to receive the impressions thereof;" or, "He hath given them the knowledge of the object of this world."

swept away; such sacred names as loyalty, religion, morality, tolerance, ruthlessly subverted; an unhallowed alliance formed between profligacy and orthodoxy on the one hand, and austerity of life and hypocrisy on the other. All the ordinary sanctions of conduct seemed enfeebled, and, whether at home or abroad, the way opened to blank Atheism, which said, not in the heart but openly, "There is no God;" to Deism, which respectfully conducted God to a chair of practical impotence in the administration of the world, utterly rejecting any possibility of revelation, politely robbing Him of any claim to a personal living power; to a general Latitudinarianism, which refused to recognize that any one particular form of religion was right, or any one manifestation of it wrong—such a system as we have lately had to encounter in London, or at least have forced to declare itself—which would include, under "the principles of religion," non-Christian systems, such as Mahomedanism, and also systems diametrically opposed to the very first principles of the Divine Author of Christianity.

But in the seventeenth century, atheism and Deism had not reached the scientific development to which they attained in the century which followed. The atheism of the Rebellion, the Restoration, and the Revolution was to a great extent the practical atheism, which had parted with God, and theoretically wished to prevent His return.

A rebellion without a restoration, or at least a revolution in the form of Deism, was the tendency of the day.

And so at the present time, there is not so much intellectual atheism to contend with, inasmuch as the current of unbelief and misbelief does not run in that direction. "The darkest word uttered by thoughtful doubt concerning the personal existence of God and man's future state, is the word 'Agnosticism,' 'We do not know.' It is not the atheist's word 'We deny.' Nor is it more than a minority of thoughtful doubters, who are content even with the position of agnosticism. The majority of doubters are as confident of the general truths of Natural Religion, as they are dubious of the special truths of Revealed Religion."[1]

Further, there is no lack of evidential work. Treatises, books, and sermons, dealing with the nature, causes, and different aspects of doubt, are plentiful and powerful; the difficult thing is to get people to listen to them, or, even more, to be able to listen to them. There must be the wish to hear and the power to hear.

It will be helpful, at all events to some, to consider things as they are. "It is assurance, it is corroboration of the faith that is in us, which you and I so pitifully need. We all indeed recoil in times of doubt from what are called 'Christian Evidences;' they seem so desperately remote from the thing itself. They are always setting us down before we have got to our goal. But intelligent and secure and satisfied confirmation of what we hold, that is another matter."[2]

It would be idle to deny that there is atheism, deliberate, successful, and splendidly equipped, around us.

[1] "Religious Doubt," by J. W. Diggle, p. 104.
[2] "Pleas and Claims," by Canon H. Scott Holland, p. 87.

It would be idle to deny that there is even more agnosticism, and a religion which, such as it is, sits very loosely to, and is impatient of, a revelation of any dogmatic system whatsoever.

But most of all, there is around us the practical atheism of a life of material gratification, limited by the horizon of this world, which aims at making this present state of things as comfortable as possible, and knows nothing of any other. There are abundant signs that the old scheme of Christian revelation is felt to be antiquated, to have lost its practical interest, to be out of date, out of touch with the times. Why should we read Old Testament history, when now we can read all the history of the world in its true philosophic bearings? Why should we read Hebrew poets and study Hebrew records, when we have others with as great or greater claims to true inspiration? Why should we puzzle ourselves about dogmatic subtleties, when men and women are starving around us; or bother our heads about the ecclesiastical polity of the first two centuries, when we have political questions of burning interest waiting for solution and demanding instant settlement? The voice of the Church, they tell us, is muffled by the dense folds of past superstition, and conditions only suitable to other times.

No doubt, revelation, as such, is unpopular in many quarters. Is it out of date or unpractical, or without a present bearing on the questions of the day?

Here surely is an investigation which cannot be without profit to all: it is a profitless and somewhat exasperating task to combat atheism, with those who are not atheists, or with those who, if they be such, are not likely to be moved by a lecture. It is a thankless task to preach a dry lecture on abstract topics in London of to-day. But surely, when there is this admitted tendency to throw off the old sanctions and the old obligations, to live without God in the world, to think we could have written a better Bible, or have devised more profitable restraints than Church obligations, more potent forces for good than the Christian sacraments, it will not be amiss, nor out of harmony with the expressed wishes of the founder of these lectures, if we try to see that revealed religion, the religion of Jesus Christ, is just as important now as ever it was; that its truth is no abstract conclusion of a logical syllogism reposing in musty treatises, with no human affinity to our throbbing life; that it is no mere elaborate system, in which we shall have to pass an examination before we are admitted to the courts of heaven, in which it is conceivable that we might do well to spend the eternity of a future state. It will not be amiss to try and show that Christianity and revealed religion are real things bound up in our life, that they are true, not merely by a process of demonstration, but because they are tragically and solemnly true, inasmuch as they are the framework of our existence, running up into it, supporting it, ministering to its development.

When we ask, is Revelation true? is Christianity true? we are not asking an abstract question which we can conduct dispassionately in consecutive numbers of the *Nineteenth Century* or *Contemporary Review*, by means of a friendly symposium,—we are asking a question which is bound up in our most intimate life.

For Christianity touches us at every turn, and affords that explanation which alone can rid us of the maddening thought that we are playing a game of chess with an unknown adversary, where a mistake is answered by a blow, and that a blow without a word.

The subject, then, which we will endeavour to consider, is the witness of human life to the truth of Revelation.

We know what Revelation says of human life; let us see what human life says of Revelation.

In the science of historical criticism a comparatively new factor has appeared in the spade of the excavator. Whereas, "the ages before the beginning of the so-called historical period in Greece had become a blank or almost a blank—they were like the maps of Central Africa made some forty years ago, in which the one-eyed monsters, or vast lakes, which had occupied it in the maps of an earlier epoch, were swept away, and nothing was put in their place,—it has been reserved for modern exploration to supply the vacant place, and to prove that, after all, the Mountains of the Moon and the lakes of the Portuguese map-makers had a foundation in fact. It has been similarly reserved for the excavator and archæologists of the last twenty years to restore the lost pages of the ancient history of civilization, and to make it clear that the literary tradition, imperfect though it may have been and erroneous in its details, was yet substantially correct."[1]

Ancient mounds, forgotten tombs, buried ruins, give up their testimony, and there it all is: that which we regarded as mythical, or legendary, or the breath of a quaint tradition, stands out as a living fact. Men acted and lived and read and wrote and painted and sang, just as history represents them. It is true; it is no legend. The life stamped upon their outward surroundings corresponds to the life which tradition has assigned to them.

[1] "The Higher Criticism and the Monuments," by Rev. A. H. Sayce, pp. 17, 18.

I claim that similar results may be discovered on behalf of Revelation, from excavations, as it were, carried out in the region of human experience.

Something like this has already been considered on a large scale.

In his famous "Analogy," Bishop Butler describes the supposed case of a man to whom, ignorant of the course of history, the great outline of Bible facts had been narrated—such as the creation, the setting apart of Israel, and the coming of the Messiah; and on his asking whether the revelations narrated in this Book were true, instead of a direct answer being given, there is put before him a succinct account of the facts of the world's history, corresponding with these, that he might compare them;—and he speaks of the great force which the joint view of both together must bring to bear upon his understanding.[1]

So, in a narrower way, it must be of great weight to any reasonable man, if, on interrogating

---

[1] Bishop Butler, "The Analogy," etc., chap. vii., sect. ii., ad finem.

experience, he finds the traces of a state of things which the Bible sets before him as a revelation from God, evidently or suggestively appearing in the circle of human experience, furnishing a reasonable explanation of certain difficulties, explaining certain facts, accounting for certain tendencies. It would be in a new sense what Tertullian speaks of as "the testimony of the soul naturally Christian."[1]

For instance, Revelation has a great deal to say about God; it represents the history of the world, and the history of every individual man, as a tapestry work, gradually being woven out by a supernatural Being, Who sits outside it all, and controls its destinies. Men and nations rapidly pass into the machine of time, and reappear as part of the pattern of history. Does human experience agree with this, or not?

We are told, again, that this is a good world ruined, and that human nature is a good nature perverted. Once more, does this correspond with facts which come under our notice?

[1] Tertullian, "Apology," chap. xvii.

The whole of Revelation is interpenetrated with the phenomena of what is called sin, the temptation to it, the effects of it, the punishment of it, the reversal of its power. Is sin an existing fact, or merely a theological spectre?

Grace, which occupies so large a place in theology, does it show any trace of its existence, except in the heated fancy of enthusiasts, or in the influence which passes through from the emotions to conduct?

It is obvious that we have here a very important inquiry. Religion claims to exercise a transforming power over a man, at every stage of his existence, and, indeed, to be the very key of the problem of human action. Do we find any corroboration of this in the records of human experience?

And where shall we look? Shall we go with the science of comparative religions, and see, what appears to be a fact, although it is sometimes denied, that no nation or people, however degraded, has been utterly deficient in the idea of God?[1] Shall we strip religion bare of the super-

---

[1] Dr. Liddon, "Some Elements of Religion," Lect. ii., sect. ii.

natural, the idolatries, the local colouring, until we find a residuum of dependence and a feeling out after a sublime ideal, common to all?

This is possible, and has already been abundantly accomplished.

But surely we may get closer even than this. To return to our first illustration.

The excavator is not content with wide and general gleanings over those spots where ancient civilizations flourished, but fastens rather on some mound or ruined temple, where tradition tells him the objects of his search will most probably be accumulated. So in looking for traces of religious experience, we will not look at the average man, in whom we should expect to find only faint and fitful vestiges of a religion which does not pretend to appeal to the low average moral level;[1] but we will investigate, if possible, the religious consciousness of a Christian, taken at a high level, remembering that spiritual things are spiritually discerned, and that the results and traces of a true Christian life, what it can effect, what it can

[1] See "Bampton Lectures," by Canon Gore, Lect. viii., sect. ii.

do, are to be looked for in those who have most developed the spiritual side of their being.

We do not search the annals of philosophy to ascertain the results of physical training, neither will we search anywhere but in the higher region of man's spiritual development, to see what religion has effected, and if it corresponds with what is presupposed and professed in the scheme of Revelation.

II.

Let us confine ourselves to-day to a brief investigation of this one point: What has the human experience of spiritual men to say to the statement propounded by Revelation; that there is a personal God, living, active, beneficent, Who interferes with and controls human actions; Who has rights and claims, and offers to be the friend and companion and protector of those that seek Him?

Has human nature found any trace of such a God? Do we find any conviction of this claim in the records of human experience and, we may add, in the testimony of our own lives ?

Looking out widely over the history of religion, we find generally that men have approached a Being outside themselves, Whom they call God, in three ways.

They felt out after a great Presence outside them; the untroubled and sacred sky was to them the unquestioned abode of God, as the earth was of man, and it opened straight through its gates of cloud and veils of dew into the awfulness of the unseen world. And they declared that this God was worthy, and they worshipped.

Or they felt within that strong, irrepressible sense of guilt, of remorse, of an eternal principle of right and wrong, and of God Who administers the laws of the universe in accordance with that principle, and they sacrificed and did acts of reparation and penitence.

Or they pondered and mused over the mysteries of life, its joys and sorrows, and they found, even if they did not know the alphabet of communion, that prayer was the means of connection with a great Being outside them, and with more or less imperfection they prayed.

Let us follow up, then, any of these three roads, in spiritually developed lives, and we shall find that human experience has discovered the very same God that Revelation made known to us as the object of religion.

(1.) See where the reverence for God expressed in worship leads the spiritual man. Worship is the expression of a homage at once complete and unlike any other, reserved for God Himself. It finds, perhaps, an unique expression in the grand liturgical hymn, where, after exhausting as it were every other cause of thankfulness, the Church cries out, "We give thanks to Thee for Thy Great Glory."[1]

Surely it is a great fact, not that the earth merely should be strewn with temples, costly and magnificent and widely diffused, but that men, the more advanced they get in spirituality, should be the more drawn to worship. An unreasoning

---

[1] See Dr. Liddon's "University Sermons," 1st series, Sermon x., p. 294, 1st edition.

enthusiasm, fashion, tradition, a thousand things, might drive the ordinary man, as we say, to go to church, but why should a man, the more he develops his spirit, more and more be impelled to reverence a Great Being outside him in worship? From the hymn of the inspired Psalmist, "One thing have I desired of the Lord, which I will require: even that I may dwell in the house of the Lord all the days of my life, to behold the fair beauty of the Lord, and to visit His temple,"[1] down to the biography of the last saint, who finds his chief delight in the worship of the altar, his fondest utterances the sacred phrases of the Bible, we find this obvious and suggestive phenomenon.

Why is it? Is it not abundantly clear that the further you mount on the golden stairs of spirituality, the more you rise above the drifting smoke and the confusing mists, the more you look out upon God?

It is true, as even the ordinary man sees, in no pantheistic sense, but in a certain and real way, that this world in its beauty is the waving garment

[1] Ps. xxvii. 4.

which conceals God. Look higher, look closer, mount up the stairs, and you look out on a Being Whom you are constrained to worship: "Thou art worthy, O Lord, to receive glory and honour and power: for Thou hast created all things, and for Thy pleasure they are and were created."[1]

The deliberate worship of the noblest lives is a testimony that at the end of spiritual investigation there is a personal God.

(2.) Take once more the sense of sin, which kindles the altars of the savage and arms his fury against his loved and best—that sense of sin which rolled up in a five-fold stream of sacrifice to Calvary, and streamed out in one flood into the great Sacrifice of the Altar.

Why is it that in those who mount up highest on the stairs of the spiritual life, this sense of guilt becomes most acute? We have had three examples of it in our own time. Listen to Mr. Keble, the saintly author of the *Christian Year*, bewailing his utter unworthiness as if he were the vilest criminal and the most degraded sinner. Listen

[1] Rev. iv. 11.

THE SENSE OF A PERSONAL GOD.

to Dr. Pusey, whose holy life even surpasses what the candid biographer ventures to record of him, speaking of himself as a loathsome leper, foul and defiled with sin.[1] Listen to the touching inscription from the "Dies Irae,"[2] put at his own wish on the tomb of one of the most saintly deans of St. Paul's.

> "Quærens me sedisti lassus,
> Redemisti crucem passus,
> Tantus labor non sit cassus."

Why is it? Can there be any other explanation than this—that the higher a man mounts on the ladder of sanctity, the more he is conscious of a "King of tremendous Majesty," Who sees not as man seeth, Who searches the very hearts and reins, to Whom he must give account.

Revelation tells us that no man can see God and live;[3] so experience corroborates it. The sight of God means death, the sense of God's presence means a sense of sin, and a true sense of sin argues

---

[1] See "Life of Dr. Pusey," vol. iii., chap. iv., by Dr. Liddon.
[2] See "Life and Letters of Dean Church," p. 350.
[3] Exod. xxxiii. 20.

God's presence. "The Crucifix," in spite of all that can be said, is no morbid craving for an imaginary consecration of asceticism. It is the medium whereby alone man can look on the majesty of God without pain. The sense of pardon, of acceptance, of forgiveness, a fellowship with Christ's suffering, such as we see, for instance, accentuated in the life of a St. Francis of Assisi, and in the humblest heart that ventures to sing only a simple hymn like "Rock of Ages," is a testimony to the truth of Revelation that the personal God, Who watches over us and claims our love, is a God Who must judge our sins, and Who wills to be the Saviour of our penitence.

(3.) We find the same corroboration in the phenomena of prayer. What a longing there has been for an answer, for a voice! what does it all mean? Is it fate? Is it jealousy? Is it malignity? Is it love? How shall the oracle be awakened, the dumb idol forced to speak?

God left not Himself without witness in the darkest time. Who shall say that no voice found its way through the stillness or penetrated the silent anguish of the dark world?

But here again, ask the spiritual man. Ask Abraham who walked with God, the friend of God, what was that Voice Which led him to give up all—his home and fatherland, and start forth a stranger in a strange land? Ask the holy writer what he meant when he said, "I value prayer so, that were I to leave all else, health, wealth, endowments, all should go, I and dear prayer would go and dwell together."[1]

Here again the spiritual man is not removed from the vulgar herd, so that from his superior height he discards prayer as an idle superstition, which an intelligent man gives up, among the childish things which he puts away.

At the end of prayer there is God. It is all true; he does not fear what so-called science may decree as to the Book of revelation. It is all true; God has spoken to him; God does speak to him. Prayer and sacraments are the avenues in which the Lord God walks in the

[1] Attributed to George Herbert.

paradise of the soul. At the end of prayer he has found that which Revelation said he would find—God as an indwelling spirit, Who hears and answers prayer, Who dwells with us and is in us. It is inconceivable that men could spend so much time and labour on prayer, if it were a mere barren exercise, to which no answer is vouchsafed.

We need not quote the Moslem on his slip of carpet, or the Buddhist at his prayer-wheel, absorbed, happy, and in earnest, unless we are prepared to admit that God, Who fully rewards with His presence those who seek Him in spirit and in truth, completely withdraws all satisfaction, all manifestation from imperfect devotion and mistaken zeal. But this would be to make the world poorer, and would seriously limit the domain of God's empire. We have tried to argue otherwise; we shall find wide and various traces of this experience which corroborates Revelation scattered up and down, in all systems true and false.

But if we search the richest fields and dig down into the experience of the believer and the true spiritual man, we shall find what existed as a faint indication elsewhere; here, at least, a deep and strong corroboration of revealed truth, far beyond a sentiment, while it cannot be accounted for as a delusion, along the three paths of worship, penitence, and prayer.

We have pushed our way, and in the lives of the highest spiritual development we have found ourselves face to face with God—Whom worship alone adequately honours, Whom penitence alone sufficiently deprecates, Whom prayer alone reaches in the language which speaks from the heart of created man to the heart of Creator God.

III.

It may be objected that this line of argument is purely subjective, and open to all the difficulties which such a course of reasoning brings with it. But, after all, it is very similar to the evidence which we accept every day from explorers and experts in unknown fields. We accept, for instance, the existence of a race of pygmies in the wilds of Africa on the testimony of one who has been there, if he be credible, even if we ourselves find it difficult to realize the possibility of their existence; or we accept the marvels of such a thing as hypnotism, although, apart from the experience of an expert, we should deem them impossible.

It has been pointed out in a book full of interest, now in all hands, that "belief is not exclusively founded on objective evidence appealing to reason (opinion),"[1] but mainly as subjective evidence appealing to some altogether different faculty (Faith). Or again, "But the individual cannot wait for this empirical determination. What is he, then, to do? The unbiassed answer of pure agnosticism ought reasonably to be in the words of John Hunter, 'Do not think—try.' That is, in this case try the only experiment available, the experiment of faith. Do the doctrine, and if Christianity be true the verification will come—not, indeed, mediately, through any course of speculative reason, but immediately by spiritual intuition."[2]

[1] Romanes' "Thoughts on Religion," Canon Gore, p. 140.
[2] Ibid. pp. 167, 168.

We come back again to the New Testament. "If any man will do His will, he shall know of the doctrine, whether it be of God."[1] And surely, even on grounds of reason itself, it should be allowed that, supposing Christianity to be of God, it *ought* to appeal to the spiritual rather than to the rational side of our nature.[2]

[1] St. John vii. 17.
[2] See Illingworth's "Bampton Lectures," Lect. v.

LECTURE II.

THE TRACES OF A FALL—WITHIN.

"I delight in the law of God after the inward man: but I see another law in my members, warring against the law of my mind, and bringing me into captivity to the law of sin which is in my members."—Rom. vii. 22, 23.

WHEN Alexander the Great had taken Tyre, and passed the mouths of the Nile, he went into the desert to consult the oracle of Jupiter Ammon. On which an ancient philosopher ventured to express curiosity as to what this great man would ask of the gods; and when he learned that his question concerned the sources of the Nile, he exclaimed, "It would have been more worthy of him, and better for us, if he had asked what is the origin of evil, for it matters little to us to know the region from which the Nile takes it rise, but it is of the last importance to know whence come the evils which overwhelm humanity."[1]

[1] Père Lacordaire, "Conférences de la Chute et de la Réparation de l'Homme," No. 64, p. 336.

I.

"Sir, didst not thou sow good seed in thy field? from whence then hath it tares?"[1] is the question which generation after generation of puzzled humanity asks at the shrine of Infallible Truth.

And the puzzle increases because they will not accept the plain statement of Revelation. There is no uncertainty there as to the general facts. Men serve divers lusts and pleasures.[2] Every imagination of the thoughts of men's hearts is evil continually.[3] They are "alienated from the life of God."[4] They are "vessels of wrath."[5] And Holy Scripture traces actual transgression to a depraved nature. "This sinful condition does not originate with matter (as some of the Greeks held) or with God, or with any personal principle, but with man himself."[6]

Holy Scripture represents man as descended from original parents, who hopelessly betrayed the

[1] St. Matt. xiii. 27. [2] Titus iii. 3. [3] Gen. vi. 5.
[4] Eph. iv. 18. [5] Rom. ix. 22.
[6] See note by Dr. Angus, on Bishop Butler's "Analogy," chap. v., sect. 5, p. 217.

true interests of humanity, and sold their birthright for a mess of pottage; that man at the beginning was something that man has ceased to be at the present day; that a catastrophe took place known ever since as the Fall, and that, " in spite of all the physical and intellectual advance which man has made, he is always and everywhere the worse for this fall."[1]

Now here the whole question bristles with difficulties. "The Fall" is not a popular subject, for many reasons.

In the first place the doctrine of "Evolution" more than holds the field; to doubt it argues an intellectual deficiency, to limit in any way its range is to run the risk of pulling off the Rupert-drop, which may just shatter the whole beautiful and logical sequence of the process.

"Man," we are told, "is descended from a hairy quadruped furnished with a tail and pointed ears, probably arboreal in its habits, and an inhabitant of the old world."[2]

[1] "Evolution and the Fall," Essays by the late Aubrey L. Moore, p. 63.
[2] Mr. Darwin, "Descent of Man," vol. ii., pp. 389, 390. See

Some go even further and contemplate primeval mud as the probable ancestor of the whole fauna and flora of this planet,[1] facts which, if they are true, hardly prepare us to associate the highest dignity with a being, who, if we are to believe in evolution, had but just emerged from the brute into the self-consciousness of the man.

But the simple doctrine of the Fall, whatever be the origin of man, takes him at a period when evolution had already done its work. And we have been reminded, "If it ever should become certain that the first man had for his mother an anthropomorphous ape, the Christian faith, as to man, his place among the creatures of God, would remain untouched. A separate creation must have invested this Adam, before his birth, with that living soul, in whose faculties lay his likeness to the Almighty Creator. No evolution can have led up to this great gift."[2]

Prefatory Note, Dr. Liddon's sermon, "The Recovery of St. Thomas," p. 11.
[1] Lord Salisbury, "Evolution," p. 41.
[2] See Dr. Liddon as above, p. 13.

No, the Church can move quite unconcerned in the presence of the doctrine of Evolution.

But further, the bugle has already sounded which recalls Evolution from a too-confident usurpation of all possible explanation of existing phenomena—a process which asks for a blank cheque on the bank of time, and which has never left the region of hypothesis [1]—a method of which one of its principal defenders says, "We accept natural selection, not because we are able to demonstrate the process in detail, not even because we can with more or less ease imagine it, but simply because we must" [2] —or which must be accepted "because it is inconceivable that there should be another principle capable of explaining the adaptation of organisms *without assuming the help of a principle of design.*" [3]

This again makes us wonder whether we have heard the last about Evolution, and whether we have been listening to the positive command of

---

[1] "Evolution," Lord Salisbury, p. 42.
[2] Weisman, quoted by Lord Salisbury, "Evolution," p. 48.
[3] Ibid. p. 49.

philosophy, rather than obeying the insistence of conclusions which demonstrably cannot be doubted. Evolution,' as applied to man, need not disturb us, it is anterior on any showing to the Bible narrative of the Fall. It may need, itself, as a theory, considerable modification.

But beyond this, the doctrine of the Fall is not palatable to those who have formed exalted notions as to the nature and possibilities of the reign of man. This we shall have occasion to notice in our next lecture, and it may be passed over here. But further, the setting forth of the Fall in the pages of Genesis, is an offence. It is ruled out of court; it must at least be allegorical and mythical, and incapable of supporting a solid superstructure reared upon it. Certainly any one who will read what a careful writer like Delitzsch says in his new commentary on Genesis, cannot fail to be struck with voices whose echoes we recognize in science and experience, and with the contemptuous unfairness of those who cover the narrative with their own flimsy creations, and then seek to involve all in a common conflagration.

Every one must have paused at some time to consider the mystery of our relation to the lower animals, to creatures generally; the mystery of food, whereby we assimilate animal and vegetable life; the relation which food and drink have to character and habits; while to us Christians, spiritual life and death centering round eating and drinking is a familiar yet utterly mysterious conception.

Whatever it may be, the narrative of the Fall is not a simple fairy story; the whole creation is implicated; man is tempted, the object of temptation is in the vegetable, the medium of temptation used by Satan is the animal world. When we consider the place the serpent has taken universally in legend, and in popular feeling; when we know the large part that the lower animals have played in idolatries, and how they have spoken to men's imaginations in the auguries, and have wonderfully entwined themselves in man's history, it seems foolish for an age, which has listened seriously to the scratch of spirits on a slate, or the vagaries of theosophy, to reject a narrative in which man is tempted and falls, by the environment of paradise, of which we know no more than is told us—instead of being tempted by the environment of modern life.

The real difficulties of the Fall no doubt lie deeper—why man should have been exposed unprotected to these three utterances, so potent and so subtle: the subverting "Why," the point-blank questioning of an acknowledged fact; the rebellious "No," the point-blank denial of an hitherto accepted truth; the fallacious "Ye shall be as gods," something better, something more promising, the deliberate substitution of another ideal,—why all posterity should be involved in the guilt, when they had no conscious share in the transgression,—whether the brood of ills which has flown out of this Pandora's box is *post hoc* rather than *propter hoc*, after the Fall rather than because of the Fall,—these are more difficult and appropriate questions. But let us rather to-day, assuming what the Bible tells us is true about this great catastrophe, excavate as it were human nature, and see if we can find any traces of it. Let us take, as before, a highly developed spiritual nature, where humanity is at its best, where there has been no conscious alienation of property which belongs to God, where there is no dismemberment of empire, or portions of life flourishing outside the control of the will, under the home-rule of inclination, and see whether, from our experience of human nature itself, there has been this great catastrophe, and if it has left any traces behind it of weakness or decay.

Let us also see, although this shall be the subject of another lecture, whether, when man reaches out to his environment, he meets with friendly or hostile forces, whether he finds the soil congenial or the reverse, whether life is easy as answering to its proper environment, or whether it is the reverse, a struggle in which excellence is gained chiefly by opposition and stored up for another state of things.

If the Bible is right, the Fall was a complete catastrophe out of which what was once, at least potentially, perfect is being reconstructed, where what was once a garden, prolific of flowers and fruit, has been exchanged for a wilderness of probation prolific of thorns and thistles.

If this is true, doubtless we shall find traces of it; if false, human nature can neglect it with as much complacency as if it were a fairy story of the nursery.

Let us see. Let us to-day interrogate human nature and ascertain for ourselves whether it is the grand thing we assumed it to be, or whether it carries in it the confirmation of Holy Scripture, which speaks of man as fallen, and the world as doomed to failure.

II.

What is man? What opens out before our analysis?

Regions surely so vast and so mysterious, that we become confused by the echo of our own footsteps, and overwhelmed by the accumulated *débris* of centuries of exploration.

Such names as Personality, Free Will, and Predestination echo and echo back into regions which no human discovery can quite reach. Memory, imagination, reason, instinct, and many others float in the air around us. Whole sciences gather round man in his complex and complicated nature; and standing back as it were to get the general impression of this supreme and apparently final possibility of creation, what do we see?

(1.) "A being at once the wonder and the scandal of the universe." What is man? we exclaim at one time in contempt, when we see his littleness beneath the greatness of the universe around him. What is man? we exclaim in wonder, when we contemplate his unique personality. What is man? we exclaim once more in horror, when we contemplate some act of incredible baseness. What is man? we reverently murmur, when we gaze at the honour conferred on him by the Incarnation.

The general impression of man, as we trace him in the pages of philosophy, poetry, and common experience, strangely and wonderfully corroborates the old history of Genesis.

Here is a being, who in power and achievement

is admittedly the lord of Creation, but one who at the same time is marked all down his history by this strange characteristic—that, left to himself, he is depraved towards every form of depravity, "a great exception in the order of nature. While every other living thing is striving for its own good, man alone is found choosing what he knows to be for his own hurt." [1]

Feebleness and an evil bias are too palpable defects to escape even the most ordinary observation, as we watch a nature so subtle and so costly, stumbling along, deflected by a feather and crushed by a straw, while it is a phenomenon which only escapes observation because it is so universal—the melancholy which broods over life, the sense of dissatisfaction and failure which moans out from the creaking machinery, in which humanity works out its appointed destiny.

(2.) But to descend to a closer examination: what do we find, at all events in the first analysis of human nature? Two main constituent parts—a

[1] "Evolution and the Fall," Essays by Aubrey L. Moore, p. 65.

corporeal and an incorporeal, the latter of which, if we examine closer, is found to be made up of two, which are respectively labelled soul and spirit. Of these the spirit would seem to be a special organ, as it were, of God-consciousness, the medium of communication with, the very temple of the Holy Ghost, which exercises a distinct function, resulting in what we call spiritual-mindedness.[1]

It is possible that it is the same faculty which we sometimes recognize in one form of its development as conscience, the subject of all religious aspirations, the object of all religious grace, the supreme guiding power in a Christian's life, through which he holds communication with the unseen world, by means of which he can walk, held in not so much by the bit and bridle of precept, as guided by the eye of a personal God.

Such, briefly, is the spirit.

Then there is a second part of the incorporeal nature, called the soul, including the feelings and impulses, and the ruling faculty, which, if sense-consciousness represents the body and

[1] See "The Tripartite Nature of Man," Heard.

God-consciousness represents the spirit, may in its turn be denoted self-consciousness—poised between the powers of the seen and the unseen world, swayed to and fro between the flesh and spirit, borne hither and thither with the tide of their conflict. It is to this that memory comes, like a troubadour of romance, to sing its lay of the olden time; or imagination comes as a travelling artist to paint its pictures; or sentiment, like the pedlar, displays its wares, under every form of excitement and delicious joy.

And then below these two regions, yet hardly inferior in dignity, and marvellously incorporated with them, is the body, with its five ministering senses, willing slaves, like the fabled genie, ready to answer to the first summons of the will, and to lay at its feet the treasures which the world has to dispose of, to those who can offer a convenient market and are ready to pay the proper price.

Here is a wonderful organization! Who can deny it? An organization in which nature is not represented in a blind, mechanical instinct, which never alters and which never goes wrong, but by a system in which everything is subordinated to a spiritualized reason, by virtue of which man has to co-operate with God in working out his own salvation, in attaining the end of life and evolving his own chief good. No beggar in receipt of a pauperizing dole, but at the end rewarded like some State-aided institution, by a grant in proportion to local outlay. With the spirit it sweeps heaven; with the soul, all cognizable things in heaven and earth; with the body it is in touch with all the treasures of the material world.

It is a unique and wonderful position. We have no difficulty in recognizing Adam, with centuries of development around him, standing sovereign and erect among the creatures of God.

But examine this in detail, and what do we find?

First of all, this strange and wonderful fact, that there is a warp in all this delicate and marvellous machinery: that in all living things there are three possible courses open to their activity— either to stay as they are, or to get better, or to get worse. Man, if left to himself, naturally and irresistibly has a tendency to get worse.[1] The whole *raison-d'être,* so to speak, of the Catholic Church depends on this; it underlies its whole scheme of spiritual provision.

Nature by itself is so bad that nothing can be done with it; it is like a crumbling medium, in which the artist in vain attempts to carve out the creation of his genius, which falls off in flakes and chips beneath the chisel; it is like the canal connecting Lough Corrib and Lough Mask, so porous in its bed that the water sinks into the earth and refuses to act as a waterway.[2]

So, Nature being thus bad, man must be born again in the Sacrament of Baptism, before he can be even capable of the higher Christian virtues; for this, he needs the constant cleansing of repentance and pardon through the precious Blood; for this, he needs constant draughts of life in sacraments.

To fail of his end, to miss his purpose, to sink back from his true dignity, he need do nothing

---

[1] See Drummond, "Natural Law"—"Degeneration."
[2] See for this illustration "Socialism," Professor Flint.

more serious than neglect. If once he fails to seize hold of the life around him, supernaturally stored for his help, he need do nothing more. The natural tendency towards degeneration will do the rest.

Here at least we have a remarkable witness to a catastrophe in the higher region of life—a nature so wonderful and so full cannot be trusted to itself; its tendency is downwards, to slip away to ruin, like a bank which has been undermined or rests on treacherous clay.

Strangely enough, human language, as we so constantly find, has crystallized for us the same idea, that whereas evil costs us nothing to commit, we only need to let ourselves go, and it is done. It is a boat which has no need either of sails or oars, or of any effort, for it has in itself winds and waves, and current and storm. Good, on the other hand, only makes its way by an effort. It is a frail bark, badly equipped, which has to beat up against wind and tide; and hence the word "virtue," that word of strength, has pushed away, or nearly so, all other meanings, and has confined itself to that force which surpasses all other, which displays itself as if it were the supreme effort of man, in which the great struggle must be used. And the struggle which ends in goodness is—human nature being. what it is, so great and so fallen—the unique exertion of strength, which, having overcome natural degeneration, proclaims itself simply as virtue, the highest form of strength.[1]

In searching once more for the traces of the Fall within our human nature, besides the strong bias towards degeneration, which is so striking, we become conscious of the traces of great disorder.

With many people the region known as the spirit is simply void and unused. We find that all spiritual perception has departed, atrophy has set in. And although, as we have been lately reminded, the nature of man is thoroughly miserable without God,[2] and feels a void which nothing can fill, yet still there is the dread "I cannot see,"

---

[1] Père Lacordaire, "Conférences de la Chute et de la Réparation de l'Homme," No. 64, p. 323.

[2] "Thoughts on Religion," Romanes, ed. by Canon Gore, p. 150.

a state surely of intense and awful pain, which points back quite as much as pain of mind or pain of body to the blow struck at the most delicate susceptibilities of human nature in the Fall, which it would be cruel to blame as sinful, and unkind to accept as normal. But apart from this, there are cases where the spirit is a ruin, where spiritual sins have been allowed to enter—envy, presumption, distrust of God,—and in the emphatic language of Holy Scripture, the Spirit who dwells within us is quenched.[1]

As with the spirit so with the soul. We know the maimed activities which underlie indolence, the perversion of life, the inability to realize its great power and responsibilities. We know what frivolity and want of earnestness can do in the aimlessness of a ruined soul.

But the phenomenon which startles us most is the phenomenon of the rebellion of the lower powers against the higher. There they are, those strange powers! How quiet and stilled they look beneath the calm surface of the well-ordered life!

[1] 1 Thess. v. 19.

THE TRACES OF A FALL—WITHIN.

The will gives its orders, the passions obey. The spirit sends down its royal message to the soul, the soul receives it, and adds all the sanction of a well-ordered reason. Memory, imagination, affection, are all controlled and subservient.

But look! As the summons of temptation begins to be heard, and the passions are roused to listen, hear the mutinous mutterings, see the sullen acquiescence, note the orders only imperfectly carried out! The storm is beginning to rise, the waves of passion roll in before the blasts of temptation and beat frantically against the wall, resolutions are scattered to the winds; the sense of self-interest, fear, respect, love of God, duty, all totter together.

The will gives its orders still, but with a faltering voice; the region of the spirit is dark, and conscience anxiously pleads, and reason stands dumb, cowering before the storm. "O wretched man that I am!" cries the tortured soul, "who shall deliver me from the body of this death?"[1]

Who is there, who has experienced this war in

[1] Rom. vii. 24.

the members (and who has not?), who can doubt the cruel nature of that blow, which left the sovereign power so weak and the subject powers so strong?

The disorder of which human nature is capable, the disorder which never allows the strongest saint to lay aside his shield and sword, the disorder which at any moment may land us in a hideous fray—all speak to us of a nature which not only inherited original sin, but also a warp of weakness and sinfulness, which, for the peace of Eden in its tranquillity of order, substituted the rebellion of nature, with its divided control and impaired authority.

But if we would see further the marks of the Fall, we must trace it not only in degeneration and disorder, but in the awful capacity for degradation, in which man has the melancholy privilege of excelling every other animal. Nero, the matricide, the debauchee, the ruin of fair promise, an embodiment of Antichrist, is a specimen of what fallen nature can be, of the depth to which it can sink: and as we pass now through the world, no longer a paradise, and see men and women toiling at an unyielding ground instead of developing its kindly growths; as we hear the groans and sighs of its suffering, and note its countless woes and its tragic sorrows; as we pass the hospital, the sick-room, the battle-field, we feel there are greater woes than these. Sadder than the sad sight of the starving poor is the sated misery of the gorged glutton; sadder than the bed of fever is the unspeakable degradation of the sensualist, who is foul in thought and loathsome in action; sadder than the sight of a poor clouded brain which God has afflicted is the sight of the drunkard wilfully depriving himself of reason and abdicating his imperial claims.

No being is so great as man in his virtues and in his fall, and looking at him sunk so low, we can come to only one conclusion: "An enemy hath done this."[1]

III.

Here we have the poisonous entail reaching down the ages in the long chain of heredity,

[1] St. Matt. xiii. 28.

leaving the taint of degeneration, the capacity for disorder, and the power of degradation, as the accumulating price for which Adam snatched at knowledge in a forbidden way.

Do not let us falsely accuse God, or think that He meant to keep man, as it were, for ever in the nursery of his childhood, and allow him to enjoy only a maimed life, from which good and evil were alike shut out. Holy Scripture does not say this, and this was not, we feel sure, the intention of God. "The external knowledge of evil, as a foe to be combated, which man was obviously intended to have, is a very different thing to the interior, sinful, sympathetic knowledge of it, which was the consequence of the Fall."[1]

Any one who knows the plague of his own heart will not need to be told that there was no progress in the Fall, save a progress downwards.

We can see, as we have tried to see in the circle of our own experience, what the Fall has really done. The same maddening power which sin and temptation exercise, on a small scale, within the

[1] Wordsworth's "Bampton Lectures," p. 208 n.

limited enclosure of our life, carried out in the great life of nations, means wars of aggression, lust, avarice, and plunder—the prolific disorder of nations which plunder for self instead of working for God.

The same degeneration which lets a man sink down through the various steps of decadence, means, on a large scale, the extermination of nationalities, such as we see again and again in the history of the world.

> "The isles of Greece, the isles of Greece!
> Where burning Sappho loved and sung.
>
> . . . . .
>
> Eternal summer gilds them yet,
> But all, except their sun, is set."

It means such a degradation as the Hebrew prophets denounced, or Juvenal satirized, or Tacitus painted. "Contrast the broken, maimed condition of single persons, and of the race, with the design of God's love for its perfection, and then, if you can, associate it with progress."[1]

Here, surely, from the interrogation of human nature, we have seen enough to assure us that

[1] Wordsworth's "Bampton Lectures," p. 209.

the Fall is no dream, and that any scheme of Evolution must make way for it, if it would account for all the facts.

Each one for himself can answer for it on the careful investigation of his own personality.

"God created man to be immortal, and made him to be an image of His own eternity. Nevertheless, through envy of the devil came death into the world: and they that do hold of his side do find it."[1]

[1] Wisdom ii. 23.

LECTURE III.

THE TRACES OF A FALL—WITHOUT.

"And unto Adam He said, Because thou hast hearkened unto the voice of thy wife, and hast eaten of the tree, of which I commanded thee, saying, Thou shalt not eat of it; cursed is the ground for thy sake; in sorrow shalt thou eat of it all the days of thy life."—GEN. iii. 17.

WE have seen in the composition of human nature, at once grand in its possibilities and pitiable in its powers of degradation, a startling confirmation of the narrative of the Fall provided for us in the book of God's revelation, which starts with man made in the image and likeness of God, and leaves him a piece of clay, buffeted by Satan and harassed with troubles, to pass away after a life of toil into the prison-house of death, which his transgression has merited.

Let us to-day go a little further in the same investigation.

I.

If man shows abundant traces of a great fall, what of the world in which he is called upon to live? Are there traces of a fall in this too? Is man placed in healthy or unhealthy surroundings?

Can he repose his crushed and wearied nature on a healing and sympathetic earth? Or has he to dread agues and fevers, and tearing beasts and piercing thorns, which drive him ever onwards with inhospitable threats, if he stays to seek repose?

He is cursed in his heredity; is he also cursed in his environment?

In pursuance of the plan we have hitherto adopted, let us first ask Revelation what it has to say on the subject; how it regards this world, which is the theatre of human action, in which generation after generation has to play out its part, until the final winding up of the ages is accomplished and the end has come.

If Revelation says but little, what it does say is significant.

Perhaps St. Paul, more than any other writer, gives us the inspired summary of the situation set up in the world by the Fall. " The creature was made subject to vanity, not willingly, but by reason of Him Who hath subjected the same in hope, because the creature itself also shall be delivered from the bondage of corruption into the glorious liberty of the children of God."[1]

"The creation was subject to failure,[2] not of its own will."

Holy Scripture does not ask us to imagine a world anterior to this calamity, an utter stranger to pain and death; the very stones we tread on give up a history, which would contradict it if, *per impossible*, it attempted such a misstatement.

But to quote some thoughtful words on the subject: " The counter-law by which the whole creation has been made subject to vanity, is to be referred to no other epoch than the fall of man. Prior to that time, all nature was lovingly obeying the laws impressed upon it by God; the herb was yielding its seed, the animal was bringing forth its kind,

---

[1] Rom. viii. 20, 21. [2] τῇ ματαιότητι.

each to be succeeded by a more numerous growth of its own species, or to make way for more highly organized types of animal or vegetable life.

"Decay meant reproduction, dissolution, development; death, a return into the general life of nature, which was to be succeeded by a more prolific emergence. All was obeying the beneficent laws of the Creator." [1]

Here may have gone on, in its perfection, that natural selection of which no man, or succession of men, in our world, as far as we know, has ever observed the whole process in any single case.[2]

While everything was thus fulfilling its end, man, we are told, strangely fell out of gear, and involved in his downfall the whole creation.

It was failure that passed over the world—an inability to secure its end, aimless pain, and aimless insult, and aimless catastrophe, exhibited the world as a wheel spinning round in vacancy, with only a partial and spasmodic connection with the motive power and final cause of the machine.

[1] Ellicott, "Destiny of the Creature," p. 10.
[2] "Evolution," Lord Salisbury, p. 50.

The difference as regards man has been expressed in one sentence.

The charge given to man was now represented by "the change of order, from the keeping of the garden to the tilling of the ground."[1]

And I ask you, is not this the brand which common observation shows us to be burned deep from some cause or another into the face of creation—Failure?

Look at that page open before us, as we gaze down from the hillside, where the sheep lie white and peaceful on the velvet slopes, and the lanes lose themselves in verdure, and the hills roll away in waves of rising and falling ground to the mountain barrier beyond; there, where the swallow darts along, and the butterfly dances in the sunbeam, and the gnats and insects weave their intricate manœuvres, and the flowers peep from the hedgerows, along which man passes to his daily work.

Beautiful and peaceful it surely is. But if we go down to examine the page, what do we find? Blight and decay, the red beak, the tearing claw,

[1] Professor Ruskin.

the struggle for existence as the very plants strive to push each other out of the way and monopolize the soil for themselves. Failure—a missing of purpose, a terrible expenditure of energy to reach a maimed result—this is written over it all.[1]

There are two cries which contend with each other above the teeming life of this earth. The one: "God made us all for good." The other: "Creation was made subject to failure not of itself."

And this is the environment in which man has to live and work. A world which inspection will show to be rightly indicated in Holy Scripture as an unhealthy world, a world incurably and radically defective, which at the best can be patched up, but in itself can nevermore be the true and final home of man, although a great restitution will take place, in the New Heaven and the New Earth, wherein dwelleth righteousness.[2]

---

[1] See sermon, "God is Love," Canon Scott Holland; "Contemporary Pulpit," vol. i., p. 4.
[2] 2 St. Peter iii. 13.

So it is by no means a barren speculation which we undertake to-day. It must largely affect our plans and modes of life, if we discover that the circumstances in which we are placed cannot be trusted; that the world is tainted; that if we rest on it, we are resting on a failure; that if we try to remain in it, it is unstable; that if we ask it to satisfy us, it is powerless to do so.

It is not an indifferent matter, whether or not our shattered and enfeebled nature reaches out and touches a perverted and treacherous environment.

II.

Taking man at his highest development, let us ask the spiritual man, the man in whom his nature is working harmoniously—where the will is resolute and makes itself respected, and the orders from on high flash through an unclouded spirit, are deciphered by reason and executed by the mental or bodily faculties—let us ask him, what account he gives of the environment in which he is working?

He will tell us, that in the region of the spirit

he is conscious of a confusing and disturbing cloud, which is known as the world, a mist as it were which gathers with great rapidity and alarming volume from life all around him; it obliterates distance, and confuses objects, and obscures the light, and makes it difficult to read the indication of God's will.

There spreads the influence, for so it is, mounting up from the lives of men, gathered thick over history, poured upwards in dense volumes from the careless lives of men, rolling in black wreaths over creatures which appeal to the appetite, so dense that, it would seem, some only lived to eat and drink, and to be comfortable. It smooths out the distances in religion and obliterates objects of faith, producing thereby one never-altering result, in body, soul, and spirit—softness, comfort, no hard outline of doctrine, no stern, unflinching morality, no ascetic rules. The world religion, the world morality, the world ideals,—these are things difficult to reconcile with the severity of the gospel of the Crucified.

Here surely is a very startling phenomenon

which meets us quite at the outset, that the spiritual man, the man who has himself entirely under control, cannot let himself go, so to speak, in the world's environment in which he is placed. While he gets good out of the world for all sorts of purposes, he has at the same time to guard against this tarnishing mist. He knows that even while he is taking in food for the machinery of life, the world with its feasting and luxury may swoop down and injure his integrity. He finds he must be rigorous and watchful with fasting and abstinence—so unhealthy is the world. While he satisfies his sense of beauty in art and music, he is conscious that he has to be watchful, that he cannot let himself go. While he carries out the end of life to which God has called him, once more, he dare not let himself go. It is a dangerous and unhealthy atmosphere, and, like the famous Italian grotto, while it strikes with its deadly vapour all that move close to its surface, it spares those who keep themselves above it.

An atmosphere so dangerous to spiritual life, is at least significant. It tells us of a time when man upset from their purpose the creatures around him, and shows us how the creatures have retaliated by vitiating the atmosphere with that taint which every Christian child renounces at the Font, under the name of the world.

But even more, we are bound to recognize this truth, when our intellectual life is feeling its way towards ideals for itself and for humanity.

We are living, we are told, now in an age, when the great Church movement is turning its attention towards social questions, towards the amelioration of the world, and the breaking down of the inequalities and injustices which so mars its equable working.

If so, surely it is of the very last importance that we should be able to answer these questions— How far can we hope to go? Is this a healthy world or not?

Many and many a generous heart is being broken, or simply ploughing the sand, because he forgets these two things.

Life is limited by death, and life is conditioned by the infinite disorder of the Fall.

What have the large majority of men got their eyes fixed upon? You may talk to them, you may interest them, you cannot divert their eyes from it for long. In one form or another, more or less, on material wealth, on the good things which the world contains.

The toil of man has amassed a good deal of capital, since the gates of Eden closed behind the expelled pair. The surface of the land, the bowels of the earth, the rivers, the trees, the air, the sunlight, all have been ransacked, and made to give up their treasures. The earth has been found to be immensely productive, and a man can become what is called rich.

But some are starving, while the world is a rich world, and they curse and mutter, and say, "We are robbed of happiness; we ought to have more of this rich world."

And some have enough, but they say they ought to have more, and that they are being cruelly defrauded of that which is a right, and which would make them happy.

And some have too much—"Never mind, riches

can buy happiness"—and they buy up pleasure after pleasure; but either it has just flitted somewhere else, or it escapes as soon as it is apparently captured.

What is it? Was this the task Adam and Eve were set to do, to set the ball of progress rolling, that a rich dividend might be proclaimed, in which fortunate shareholders should have the lion-share and every one else quarrel and languish and scheme for it?

What did our Blessed Lord say to it all?

He was asked more than once what He would do, what He would advise. A young man had not, or thought he had not, his proper share of an inheritance. He appealed to our Blessed Lord, Who simply answered, "Man, who made Me a judge or a divider over you?"[1]

The Jews appealed to Him as to the tyrannical injustice of the Roman Empire, which had subjected all the lands and demanded a tribute, which outraged their religious scruples and conflicted with their sense of justice.

[1] St. Luke xii.

They, too, asked our Blessed Lord what they should do, and He simply said, "Pay; it is Cæsar's right, and while you are paying Cæsar, do not forget God."[1]

He Himself, to Whom all conditions were open, deliberately chose that of poverty, and, what is more, which people seem strangely to forget, praised poverty, blessed poverty, inculcated poverty. What did He mean?

He meant that this was an unhealthy world; that all this accumulation of resources might be a distinct curse, if it led men to forget the true nature of the world in which they lived. It is in no sense permanent; its value is in its fitting men for another state, and "a man's life" (and mark you, this applies to the discontented poor as well as to the covetous rich), "consisteth not in the abundance of the things which he possesseth."[2]

Surely we are making a tremendous mistake if we forget this.

When we talk of improving man's condition, what do we mean?

[1] St. Matt. xxii. 17-21. [2] St. Luke xii. 15.

You would be conferring a doubtful advantage on a dweller in the tropics, if you persuaded him to live like a European, and not to think of the climate, which should be the first and last consideration in laying out his rule of life, under these circumstances.

Are we quite sure that, in our scheme for social amelioration, we have put the horizon high enough?

The air is full of denunciation of the rich—why? It is full of commiseration of the poor—why?

Because the one have, and the other have not the desideratum of life; or perhaps, put more fairly, because the one have more, and the other have less, than their share of the good things of this world.

The socially good man—is it possible to delineate him? He is the man who would have a comfortable competency, with few cares and plenty of leisure; his duties would be mapped out for him and enforced by a careful Government; he has no call to give to the poor—that would pauperize them, and in an ideal State there would be no poor;

his share of contribution to public schemes is regulated by a rate; he has no call to cultivate poverty of spirit, meekness, or patience; if his immediate environment is not such as to secure his proper development, "the getting of himself out" to the best advantage, he must agitate and complain. We have often met such people in the different spheres of life, excellent, law-abiding, peaceful citizens, and yet, in a sense, we are free to confess that they do not represent man at his best.

They are to a great extent earth-bound; they have an ideal—that earthly well-being, not necessarily for self but for the community, is the goal of existence, and a whole batch of the higher mechanism of life becomes useless, and whole groups of Christian virtues become otiose or even anti-social.

Why should a man take up his cross, if he ought to claim as a right his full development? Why should a man deny himself, when he must simply make the best of a properly constituted environment?

Do not mistake me; all honour to those who are labouring to make the way of life less full of temptation, less full of wrong and disabling conditions. But at the very best, when we have done all, our home can never be more than a shifting tent, and our surroundings to the last degree unhealthy and perilous. The time can never come when the road to heaven will be anything else but strait and narrow, or the enemies who beset us be materially diminished; self-denial, patience, the cross, will always be necessary.

The very man we were thinking of just now, may, out of his smug self-satisfaction, have a larger share of the rich spirit, denounced in the Bible, than he who has more claims to be considered absolutely rich, but has learned to be poor in spirit. The man who gives way to the luxury of grumbling and discontent may breathe forth more of the poisonous spirit of disabling riches than either, where he sits brooding over his few pence and his bare home, believing himself to be robbed of his rights, and hugging to himself the imaginary riches which he considers ought to be his.

Do not let us forget that when our Blessed Lord denounced the covetous and rich, and pronounced His woe on riches, He did not praise as the opposite a competence, but poverty.

But now when men denounce riches, it is that there may be a larger and wider distribution of what, after all, is the main thing to live for, as enabling a man to develop himself. Whereas poverty and the poor are things not even to be named; so a modern writer speaks of "the working man," or as it was in other days the loftier fashion to call him "the poor," as if the term "poor" could only be used by a man who forgot that it was a badge of social indignity.

"A man's life consisteth not in the abundance of the things which he possesseth." We shall find that we have missed due proportion, if we put environment first and man second. The environment of man cannot beyond a certain point be made beneficial to the pilgrim on his road to heaven.

Even when it is most successful, and life has been made as easy to him as possible, the evils which beset him only change their character; and certainly, of all deadening spiritual influences, a competency, where everything is smooth and responsibility reduced to a minimum, is the most deadening.

You may produce a more equable world, with less startling incongruities and less heartless injustice. But if the Church in the mean time has been preaching politics instead of religion, justice instead of holiness, the kingdom of earth instead of the kingdom of heaven, she will be turning unimproved men into improved conditions, or, at the best, men abundantly capable of making the best use of the house furnished and prepared which is built on the sand, while the wind is already beginning to freshen and the tide is turned, and in a few hours there will be a surface rippled with waves and white with foam, where before was the house built on wrong principles, on an unstable base.[1]

[1] See Bishop of Durham, "The Incarnation and Common Life," p. 333.

It would be an immense thing if, in all the love and energy which is being expended, we remembered this simple truth—we are legislating for fallen men, in an unhealthy and stifling environment.

Yet once more: if the spiritual man is confronted by a deadly environment known as the world, and the intellectual man is baffled by unhealthy and unstable conditions, so the lower side of man—the physical man—is confronted by a survival of the Fall, which he cannot ignore, known as pain.

This has been one of the mysteries which has most baffled man. Why is it allowed? Whence does it come? Why is it so unequally distributed? Will it ever be reduced to a minimum, to a vanishing point, by human resource and discovery?

And I may remind you once more, that ready as He ever was to alleviate it and remove it, yet that Jesus Christ never seemed to contemplate or wish for the entire removal of pain, any more than of poverty, as things are.

The Epicurean had said "Fly from it," the Stoic said "Ignore it," Jesus Christ said "Use it." And it requires no great penetration to see what distinct advantages have gathered round pain, turning what to man was, in the first place, penal, into corrective.

I do not speak now of the prophylactic use of pain, or of its disciplinary virtues, but as the mother of some of the most splendid graces which crown humanity. And we must remember, with some awe and wonder, that this age in which we live has seen some of the greatest strides in the direction of remedying pain: the scientific use of anæsthetics, for instance, which has made whole systems of relief possible, which could not be attempted before, and has robbed accident and disease of a great deal of their terror. What does it mean? Who are we, that we should be spared so much outward suffering? Does it mean, that we may be in danger, if we are not careful, of losing some discipline which should be ours? The sense of ease and the fear of hardness, as they spread their influence wider and wider, may only too easily damage the integrity of life. We must watch, and be careful. God knows that, cushioned and guarded and scientifically watched as we may be, there is still pain enough and to spare for our discipline and correction; only, while we drink of the stupefying draught which our Blessed Lord refused, let us remember, that hardness, pain, the cross, self-denial, were some of the words most frequently on His lips, as He looked out over the Christian character.

This is what the fallen world would have to offer to man. He, while refusing to take us out of these conditions, softened and blessed them all.

Out of the world with its temptations, He brought the Crown; out of poverty with its disabling cares, He brought the kingdom; Pain He elevated into a Cross, which the sufferer, if he willingly bore it, would find at the last was bearing him.[1]

III.

Are we, then, to look for no progress, no improvement, and cease to work for any?

Is the world so incurably bad, so honeycombed with the effects of the Fall, that it never can be altered?

---

[1] "Si libenter crucem portas portabit te" ("Imitatio Christi," ii, 5).

It would be untrue and wrong to say so. There is a progress, and we are told to look for a progress. The creature itself, with its upturned head, is in hope of better things, but the progress must be in man.[1]

A humanity which is alive with Christ, can alone develop the world in a right way, otherwise it is but to load the foundations and weigh down the walls, already too much for that on which they rest, —to build a house as a permanence, where the wise man can but linger in a movable tent.

We could not make a greater mistake than to suppose this world to be so incurably bad that it is not worth thinking about, and that nothing can be done with it.

Just as the body which we so much mar has been for ever dignified as being the tabernacle of the Incarnation, so this world which we so much disfigure was once made very good by God. And He gave it into the hand of man; He allowed it to be his discipline, while he was developing its resources.

[1] See Rom. viii. 19.

So long as we remember that it is a fallen world, and that as our own good actions need the merits of Christ, so its development needs the sanctification of God; so long we may go fearlessly on in the path of progress, and rescue from the clutches of Satan, and the corruption of a bad use, this beautiful Creation of God, once perfect, now studded with imperfections and dangers.

And if we may never hope to make it perfect ourselves, at least we may strive to make it an environment in which man may live with a minimum of danger and a maximum of good.

LECTURE IV.

THE PHENOMENA OF SIN.

"For we know that the law is spiritual: but I am carnal, sold under sin."—ROM. vii. 14.

THERE can be no doubt about one phenomenon at least, which characterizes revelation from one end to the other, and that is the sense of the existence of sin as a powerful influence, which has shaped and directed the course of religion from the very first, and with which anything which claims to be in the true sense a religion must deal, if it is to satisfy the inmost needs of the heart of men.

So much is this the case, that men have accused Christians of inventing the idea of sin only for the purpose of remedying it;[1] and a pushing materialism is always trying to represent it as a theological bugbear, which seems to give weak souls an

[1] Dr. Liddon, "Some Elements of Religion," p. 129.

exquisite thrill of horror, while they imagine everything they do to be wrong.

However this may be, we accept it as a testimony that the existence of a disorder called sin is looked upon as inseparably bound up with Scripture teaching, by those who reverence its precepts, and by those who shape their conduct by them.

I.

The whole scheme, indeed, of Bible history is little else but a working out of the course of the disease, and of the remedy for the disease, which we know respectively under the names of the Fall and the Redemption.

We are told that there was a severance of the original relationship between God and man. That the knowledge of sin, latent in the heart, was deepened by the elaborate system of the Mosaic law, with its "Thou shalt not," and its constant witness to human defilement.

We are shown how this sense of alienation from God and human depravity, was deepened by the voice of the prophets, quickening the consciousness of guilt, until sin was bruised and beaten down, in the person of the Divine representative of man, who, sinless Himself, took upon Him the sin of the world, that He might take it out of the way, nailing it to His cross, and that now it exists as a curbed and broken power, but still strangely powerful, only by the consent and permission of man, who can so abuse, to his own hurt, the marvellous gift of free-will.

So that the point that we have to consider to-day is not so much the existence of evil in its generic sense, which we have been really considering in the last two lectures, but the existence of a specific evil called sin.

For there may be a sense of evil without the sense of sin, a confession of a missing the end of life, and of moral declension, still without the complete sense of what we mean by sin.

There are plenty of men who will ask anxiously, What can I do to improve myself and correct my habits? Not so many, who ask with fear and trembling, "What must I do to be saved?"

And here it becomes natural to ask for a closer

definition of sin, for something which differentiates it, and makes it recognizable as the great foe of humanity.

Sin has been described as lawlessness,[1] "something said and done in contradiction to the eternal law,"[2] "intentional contradiction in thought, word, or deed, of the perfectly Holy will of God,"[3] or "the robbing God of His due,"[4] the underlying thought in all these being a transgression against a personal God, Who upholds and administers law, Who claims rights and dues from His creatures, and Who is necessary to their full and perfect development.

The history of sin in the Bible, is the history of the break with God, of the disorder which followed, of the refusing a known standard of goodness, and introducing an unnatural state, by an independence of God, which is fatal to true natural development.

Obviously, an idea so ingrained in the Bible,

[1] 1 St. John iii. 4. [2] St. Augustine.
[3] See Dr. Liddon, "Some Elements of Religion," p. 153.
[4] "Cur Deus Homo," chap. ii. See also "On the Christian Doctrine of Sin," by Canon Gore, appendix to "Lux Mundi."

which runs as a plot through the whole system of revealed religion, if it is not an invention, or at least an exaggeration, must be largely traceable in the records of human experience. And this is the point which we must proceed to investigate.

II.

If we take a wide outlook there are three places where we might excavate experience and investigate the traces of sin: Human religion, Human experience, as expressed in representative writings, and Human language.

(a) The most striking and the most obvious expression of sin in the religions of the world is the widespread system of sacrifice, culminating, as the most efficacious of all, in human sacrifice, in which human nature, feeling itself estranged from God, reaches out pleading hands into the darkness, and by pain, by self-denial, by blood-shedding, tries to do away a sense of alienation and guilt, which may not be appeased.[1]

It may be that large and flourishing systems

---

[1] Wordsworth, "The One Religion," p. 167.

of religion have appeared, like Islam, with a very slight apparent sense of sin;[1] yet it is there, as the only adequate explanation of the austerity of fasting, which exists in that system; or with a very inadequate sense of sin, regarding it more as a misfortune than an offence against God, as in Buddhism;[2] still it is there, if it centres in self-perfection rather than in God.

In spite of whatever exceptions and drawbacks we allow, in taking the general estimate, which is all we aim at now, undoubtedly it is there, if we look far enough for it, in the sense of alienation from God which underlies rites of propitiation and whole systems of atonement.

It is the voice of the suppliant in the dark groves, where the altar smokes with blood, and only forms of vengeance and hatred look out upon him from the darkness.

It is the sense of inward corruption, common to Jew and Gentile, the voice of Nature, "the testimony of the soul, naturally Christian,"[3] which

---

[1] Wordsworth, "The One Religion," p. 262.   [2] Ibid. p. 287.
[3] See Tertullian, "De Testimonio Animæ."

wails forth in the well-known words of Micah: "Wherewith shall I come before the Lord, and bow myself before the high God? Shall I come before Him with burnt offerings, with calves of a year old? Will the Lord be pleased with thousands of rams, or with ten thousands of rivers of oil? Shall I give my firstborn for my transgression, the fruit of my body for the sin of my soul?" In his despair man witnesses to a craving for God, even while he fails to hear the answer which soothes His children: "He hath shewed thee, O man, what is good; and what doth the Lord require of thee, but to do justly, and to love mercy, and to walk humbly with thy God?"[1]

(β) The testimony of the best minds is no less remarkable, as expressed in their writings. The melancholy which sighs forth on the breeze in those sad words of the tragedian, "Best of all is it never to have been born, or, when we are born, speedily to depart whence we came,"[2] is a witness to a deep-seated despair.

[1] Micah vi. 5.
[2] "Μὴ φῦμαι τόν ἅπαντα νικᾷ λόγον τὸ δ', ἐπεὶ φανῇ, βῆναι κεῖθεν

"All men, both as individuals and public bodies, are prone to sin,"[1] says the historian. Aristotle has told us that man left to himself, is depraved in every form of depravity (πρὸς ἁπάσαν ἀκολασίαν). There is the oft-quoted line of the poet, "Video meliora proboque, deteriora sequor,"[2] while we detect, behind the brilliant prose of Tacitus and the keen satire of Juvenal, an outraged sense of propriety, as if human nature were sore at the very recollection of the foulness of the vice which crushed down natural dignity.

Or listen to the wail of Indian philosophy, "The earth has been submerged, and the very gods have fled from their places. In such a world as this, what is the use of the enjoyment of pleasures, if he who has fed on them has to return again and again?"[3]

ὅθεν περ' ἥκει πολὺ δεύτερον ὡς τάχιστα." Soph., "Œdipus," Col., 1225.

[1] "Πεφύκασί τε ἅπαντες καὶ ἰδίᾳ καὶ δημοσίᾳ ἁμαρτάνειν." Thucyd., iii. 45, 9.

[2] Ovid, "Met.," vii. 24.

[3] Note the dread of a new birth into this world, "The Vedânta Philosophy," Max Müller, p. 51; on sacrifice, see "Physical Religion," pp. 106, 110.

Or listen to the appeal to the gods of nature: "Let not one sin, after another, difficult to be conquered, overcome us; may it depart together with greed."[1]

(γ) If we examine human experience, as crystallized in language, we shall find the same testimony.

In Hebrew,[2] in Greek, in our English equivalents, sin stands confessed, as an injury, as a moral disorder, as a stumbling, a missing the mark, a fascination amounting to witchcraft, a blemish, a tendency or perversion of the will from the right way, a rebellion, a deviation from the right path.

Wherever we look around us in experience, there are abundant testimonies of the great moral disorder, which leaves a sense of guilt where no outward law is broken; a sense of injury, where no human friend has made a complaint; a sense of sadness, which no self-satisfaction can overcome.

---

[1] "Physical Religion," Max Müller, p. 319.
[2] See Dr. Liddon, "Some Elements of Religion," p. 153.

III.

But we should expect to find the greatest and most characteristic examples of the sense of sin, after all, in the experience of the spiritual man—a man, that is, in whom that part of his being most sensitive to heavenly influences is most highly developed; and once more I would draw your attention to this phenomenon.

For it is a fact at least worth noticing, that if we would seek for the most utter and complete statement of the extreme sinfulness of sin and the misery which it inflicts on the heart, we must search in the lives of the saints. So St. Francis of Assisi, when his possession of real modesty was put to the test by Brother Matteo, answered, " Thou wishest to know why it is I whom men follow? Thou wishest to know? It is because the eyes of the Most High have willed it thus: He continually watches the good and the wicked, and as His most holy eyes have not found among sinners any smaller man, nor any more insufficient, and more sinful, therefore He has chosen me to accomplish the marvellous work which God has undertaken: He chose me because He could find no one more worthless, and He wished here to confound the nobility and grandees of the world."[1]

In our own time, some have been almost scandalized by such language as this, in the biography of a holy man, where he speaks of himself as follows: "I am scarred all over and seamed with sin, so that I am a monster unto myself. I can feel only of myself like one covered with leprosy from head to foot;"[2] on which, and on similar expressions in the lives of the saints, his biographer remarks, "The truth, of course, is, that with a nearness to God comes a new and exacting standard of sin and holiness."

They are the expression of the same feeling which actuated the saint of old, "I have heard of Thee by the hearing of the ear: but now mine eye seeth Thee. Wherefore I abhor myself, and repent in dust and ashes."[3]

---

[1] "Life of St. Francis of Assisi," Sabatier, chap. xi. ad init.
[2] "Life of Dr. Pusey," Dr. Liddon, vol. iii. p. 96.
[3] Job xlii. 5, 6.

Let us examine in such conditions as these the nature of sin, and see whether Revelation is true, when it represents it as so serious a thing, that all God's dealings with man are more or less concerned with it; that it shaped even if it did not cause the greatest event the world has ever seen, when, not only "for us men," but "for our salvation," our Lord Jesus Christ " came down from heaven, and was incarnate by the Holy Ghost of the Virgin Mary, and was made man."[1]

(1) If they are interrogated thus, the lives of the saints tell us this, that, first of all, they are conscious of a failure to reach an ideal; that there is a struggle going on ever within them, with a form of ἀνομία which hinders them from attaining to that which, according to the nature of things, is absolutely and eternally right.

It is strange, this intense difficulty of being good.

We might have thought, for instance, that if a man had once thoroughly grasped the fact that thoughts and imaginations cannot be allowed to

[1] Nicene Creed.

stray without any control; that there is no common land in the limited area of human life absolutely outside all restraint, where every roving traveller may pitch his tent—that if this were once realized and determined, the matter was done. But instead, what difficulties are experienced, what life-long practice is necessary and what agonizing failures are encountered in "bringing into captivity every thought to the obedience of Christ."

Uncharitableness, selfishness, unregulated life—surely to have marked these defects is to remedy them! Why, then, this humiliating struggle protracted through a lifetime with doubtful issue and scant success?

Surely to have put before us such simple models for imitation as the gentle, the meek, the joyful, the peaceful, the humble, means a speedy and complete realization of our aim within the sphere of human action! Why, then, these crude counterfeits, these wretched shams, these mixed and adulterated forms of good?

The extreme powerlessness of human nature to eradicate evil is a startling and painful phenomenon.

It lies at the base of a fundamental Christian doctrine, which we know as Justification.

This great doctrine has suffered so terribly from a cruel and disastrous perversion that we do not always stop to give it its full working value.

It has come to be believed that the depravity of human nature is such, that it is foolish and wrong to attempt to do any form of meritorious action; that the most dangerous form of sin is that which can be labelled as good works; that Christ alone can and will do all for us; that what we do ourselves is an indifferent matter, even if it does not do absolute harm, by setting up an idea of merit: whereas the truth may be represented perhaps by this simple figure.

We human beings are like children striving to produce a work of art which can satisfy an artist. If we are able to do anything at all, it is by striving our very utmost, and using the help liberally supplied by the artist himself, who not only supplies us with means and material, but who helps us with his own hand, and works in us, and with us, until, by doing our very utmost—

that is essential—and by working with him, we are able to produce something which appears to us artistic.

But, then, we fail to realize that what we think to be good is only relatively, not absolutely, good; that is to say, it is "good for us," with our imperfect powers and defective education. And in order to be fit for the Master's use, and be made ready to be accepted by Him, it must be transformed by the merits of the Master Himself; He must transform every line and modify the whole treatment, so that what was relatively good, or good for us, becomes absolutely good when covered and transformed with the merits of Christ.

It is a strange and startling testimony to the power and universality of sin, that those who are most conversant with high and spiritual ideals feel an antagonism and an inaptitude within them which make the realization of those ideals impossible, without the preventing power of Christ and the subsequent transformation which takes place, whereby, when crowning our merit, He crowns His own priceless gifts.

(2.) Once more, if we interrogate the higher lives of the saints, besides this failure to reach an ideal, we shall find a sense of injury and slight being done to a person.

There is not only the ἀνομία which violates eternal laws by failing to reach them, but there is the ἀνομία which daily and hourly is violating little personal laws, which loyalty to a friend requires should be performed.

This is a phenomenon seen most distinctly in the saintly life, because, as we have been lately reminded, "moral affinity is needful for the knowledge of a person,"[1] and those who would most seek to know the mind of Christ, and most are guided by His eye, are most conscious of the terrible breaks and defects in the perfectness of the intercourse between the soul and God.

Take such positive precepts as Prayer, Fasting, and Almsgiving, which are enjoined in the Sermon on the Mount. Not only is the Christian shamed by his strange and inexplicable incapacity for spiritual exercises, or by the rebellion of his weak

[1] Illingworth, "Bampton Lectures," p. 113.

flesh, but he is humbled and confounded by the vision of One Who spent whole nights in prayer for him, Who wrestled during forty days' fast with the tempter, to secure our immunity when attacked, Who spared nothing, not even the glory which He had with the Father, when He came to redeem us.

The sense of unworthiness, ingratitude, almost unkindness to a personal Saviour, is a very strong feature in the sense of sin. That sin should have dominion over us in the face of the cross and under the love of the Crucified, adds to its indignity and increases its disgrace.

It is a phenomenon which we are well acquainted with—that sense of sin, as a blow struck against a personal friend, which will give the sinner no rest, until, quite apart from starting afresh and turning over a new leaf, he steals up to God, and puts himself at the foot of the cross, and says, "Against Thee only have I sinned, and done this evil in Thy sight."[1] "Lord, I love; I would love more warmly. Lord, I believe; I would believe more

[1] Ps. li. 4.

firmly. Lord, I grieve; I would grieve more deeply."

(3.) And there has already opened out a further sense of impotence, of powerlessness against sin. Here are men striving against it with every faculty strung to resist, yet fain to confess the difficulty they feel in overcoming; and yet, for all that, men and women all around us are not only neglecting the ordinary safe-guards of religion, but sailing on the flood-tide of temptation with full sails and deliberate course towards the rock of perdition. The difficulty of being good, the utterly unsatisfying nature of the best life, in view of what it might be, is a strange comment on the easy-going life and neglect of precaution all around us.

Would that the saints of God could give some little sense of sin to this generation!

It is in vain that crime is diminished, if immorality is increased; it is vain that vice is driven back from its coarser outward aspects, if it is driven in with a more terrible malignity.

The testimony of the spiritual man is that, try what he will, sin is almost too much for him.

"Nevertheless, my feet were almost gone; my treadings had well-nigh slipt."[1]

How, then, are we to account for the security which makes temptation for itself, and contemptuously despises supernatural aids?

Are we to conclude that the higher spiritual refinements are gone, in such cases, and that spiritual mortification, painless and deadly, has set in? Or that the testimony of the saints is exaggerated and unreal?

There can be little doubt that unassisted human nature is quite overmatched in the struggle with sin.

IV.

It cannot be repeated too often that we are in danger of quite misunderstanding the meaning of such things as the Dogmatic Faith, Holy Scripture, on which it rests, and Sacramental Grace.

There is no virtue in any mere series of definitions, if they only represent the views and opinions of a party; there is no particular value

[1] Ps. lxxiii. 2.

in a sacred book, beyond a literary charm, if it be not inspired and be not true; there is no particular value in sacraments, if they are merely graceful symbols and empty charms.

But when a Creed asserts, "This is the way of safety," and the Holy Scriptures act as a guide and a lamp; when sacraments impart grace, as well as symbolize it, we can see how the very spiritual storehouse which surrounds us bears witness to the weakness and danger of unassisted human nature.

Sin is a great mistake; to admit it, and to listen to it, is to take an utterly and entirely wrong view of life. Everything is inverted. "Neither is God in all his thoughts" may be taken to represent the broken unity between God and man, which the saint deplores and tries to rectify, which the sinner is only dimly conscious of.

Sin is a great catastrophe; it is a rebellion in life, which sooner or later leads the soul back from the service of Christ. Painfully and laboriously the life strains after perfection, against which the passions protest and human indolence rebels.

Sin is a great loss. "O Lord, make me what I might have been, had I never sinned!" is the prayer of the saint; while the sinner foolishly thinks that he is going to repair by some last and supreme effort the ravages of years and the licence of a lifetime.

Every one, in whatever religious state he may be, feels something of those dread symptoms which still linger about sin, even in a redeemed world; but the spiritual man feels them most keenly, as he has his eye more fully turned on the spiritual possibilities of goodness.

It has been said "there are two things a genuine Christian never does: he never makes light of any known sin, and he never admits it to be invincible."[1]

If we have any clear vision of this terrible bar and hindrance, let us do our best to neutralize it, in the circle of our own lives.

Rare as a purely good action is, we at least may strive to purify our motives, and eradicate that love of self which does so much havoc. We need

---

[1] Dr. Liddon, "Some Elements of Religion," p. 164.

not leave our ideals, but quicken our energies to reach them.

Let us aim more at that personal love of a Present God, which can be obtained by opening up, and keeping free, all the channels by which He visits our soul, such as Prayer, Meditation, and Sacraments, by asking His constant and never-failing help, which He is always more ready to give than we to ask.

"Prayer and sin cannot exist together,"[1] they mutually thrust each other out. And sin cannot exist beneath the arms of the Cross. There He hangs to destroy, not only the penalty, but the power of sin.

Yet it still remains a force which no one can despise; no formula will get rid of it; we cannot compound for it by attendance at church, or by beautiful music, or by Bible phraseology, or by mere confession, or by systems of resolutions. It always has been and always will be a difficult matter to be good.

If before Christ came, it was, so to speak,

[1] Dr. Liddon.

impossible,[1] if it is possible now, as we believe it to be, it is and always must be difficult. We cannot expect, we should fear that we were off the right track if we found it to be so, that sin, which has been the underlying stratum of the whole economy of Redemption, should cease to annoy us, or to appeal to our watchful vigilance.

Adam and his fall, the Law of Moses in its sense of guilt, the prophets with their stern voice, the cross with its sombre shadow—all speak of this one word—sin.

And the heathen, with his instinctive sense of loss and alienation, and his touching expression of it; the lives and intellects of the representative men in past ages; the testimony of language itself—all bear witness to the same dread power of sin.

While the spiritual man from his watch-towers, whither he has mounted to scan the heaven, tells us, that this baffles his efforts and clouds his observation.

---

[1] "Διὸ καὶ ἔργόν ἐστὶ σπουδαίου εἶναι," Aristotle, "Nic. Eth.," ii. 9, 2.

He cannot do the thing that he would.[1] He is ashamed of the very privileges which he is permitted to share in all his defilement. He proclaims the utter inability of man to be just with God, and still, after eighteen centuries of Christianity, feels constrained to say with the Psalmist, "They are all gone out of the way, they are altogether become abominable: there is none that doeth good, no not one."[2]

[1] Gal. v. 17.   [2] Ps. xiv. 4.

LECTURE V.

THE PHENOMENA OF TEMPTATION.

"And He said unto them, I beheld Satan as lightning fall from heaven."—St. Luke x. 18.

Closely connected with the origin of evil and the traces of a Fall, in human nature and in its environment, we cannot fail to be struck with a phenomenon—of which Holy Scripture, history, poetry, human experience, are all full—known as Temptation.

How is the inducement to commit what is undoubtedly wrong, and sometimes obviously and immediately disadvantageous, brought about?

How is it that man with his reason is worse off than a brute with his instinct? and that a life which is not governed by principle and guided by efforts seems destined to fall almost automatically under the power of adverse influence?

I.

Holy Scripture has one consistent answer, which, from end to end of the sacred writings, never varies, and is woven into the very thread of the narrative—that evil suggestion for the most part comes from a supernatural Power outside us, known as the Devil and Satan, not omnipotent, not himself omnipresent, but nevertheless with a power and pervading influence which few can resist and none can escape; who works on human free-will weakened by centuries of feeble connivance, being always able to reckon, at least, on two active allies, which, under the name of the World and the Flesh, fight his battles and promote his victories.

It will be hardly necessary to point out the very large part which this plays in Holy Scripture.

We are sometimes told that it is impossible to ask a man seriously to believe in a Devil—that to do so is to go back to the infancy of the world; that a devil with horns and hoofs is all very well for the mediæval nursery, diseased by fairy legends and the myths of prehistoric ages.

Picturesque allegory, we are told, has always had to pay the penalty of its dramatic force, and to submit to the unreasoning identification of evil with the serpent, or of the principle of evil with a personal agent. We never are far removed, men tell us, from the poetic sentiment which deifies its impression, which hears in the thunders the roll of the chariots of God, in the splash of the fountain the whisper of the water-nymphs, in the rustle of the grove the tripping of the Dryads.

It is natural enough, we are told, to personify the fiery suggestions of evil which surge and bubble in our turbid mind, until they seem to stand outside us as active agents, and the throbbing in our ear becomes a voice speaking to us, and the evil desires of our hearts the suggestion of an alien power, which marshals the attractive sights and sounds of the world until they become the impact of a seductive foe, who smites with a gloved hand and stabs with a golden dagger.

This may be so, but it is impossible to reconcile it with Holy Scripture.

It is a person with clearly defined titles and

modes of action, who, identified as the serpent, as the New Testament seems to make clear, manipulates the Fall, who, under his title of Satan, is discussed in the Book of Job, who as an evil spirit molested Saul, injured David, deceived Ahab; the name Satan occurring in four books in its narrow significance, in eight passages in its broad sense of " adversary." [1]

But what is most remarkable is this: the later we get in the history the clearer are the statements as to the personality of the Evil One; so that such a notion, so far from being the product of a rude and uncultivated age, is spoken of with every sign of approval, and is adopted without a word of caution or disparagement by our Blessed Lord Himself. So much so, that we seem driven at last to this dilemma: if Satan as a personal agent is only the creation of years of unreflecting misapprehension, of allegorical and poetical fancies, aggravated and complicated by a Babylonian demonology brought back from that paradise of critics—the Captivity,—then either

[1] Hutchings, "The Mystery of the Temptation," p. 74.

our Blessed Lord did not know that which a more enlightened age can see and appreciate without an effort, or, knowing it, He used, as the phrase is, an accommodation that He might not shock Jewish prejudice, or spoil the effect of a wholesome allegory.

This has been urged upon us again, in a fragment of a very remarkable and interesting book: "If Christ knew that the facts were not due to devils, He may also have known it was best to fall in with the current theory, rather than to puzzle the people with a lecture on pathology. If He did not know, why should He, if He had previously 'emptied Himself' of omniscience? In either case, if He had denied the current theory, He would have been giving evidence of scientific knowledge or of scientific intuition beyond the culture of His time; and this, as in countless other cases, was not in accordance with His method, which, whether we suppose it Divine or human, has nowhere proved His Divine mission by foreknowledge of natural science."[1]

[1] "Thoughts on Religion" (Romanes), edited by Canon Gore, p. 181.

We certainly must be prepared to find that a doctrine such as the Divine Kenosis, cannot be kept only for selected cases. Most of us agree with the comment made on this statement by the editor: "The emphasis which Jesus Christ lays on diabolic agency is so great, that if it is not a reality, He must be regarded either as seriously misled about realities which concern the spiritual life, or else as seriously misleading others, and in neither case could He be even the perfect Prophet."[1]

The testimony of our Blessed Lord may be regarded as bringing to a focus the consistent attitude and language of Holy Scripture.

If we are jealous of an encroachment of the supernatural, if we fix our eyes on Oriental superstition, and deprecate any approach to a coordination of good and evil powers, of course we are at liberty to do so—only we cannot with any show of reason claim Holy Scripture as being on our side, which asserts the existence and active opposition of a Personal agent of evil, who

[1] Note by Canon Gore on "Thoughts on Religion," p. 180.

characteristically makes himself felt in what is known as Temptation.

The question for us to decide to-day, or rather to examine, is this—whether we find any corroboration of this persistent attitude of Holy Scripture in the region of human experience, whether recorded in history or admitted in the common consent of everyday experience.

II.

It may not be easy to trace the sign of Satan's presence in history without being imaginative or even fanciful. We might be pardoned if we recognize in the strange deification of human passion and lust, of cruelty and treachery, the hand of one who knows how to manipulate a lie and foster a delusion to the ruin of men's souls.

(1.) The mystery of the oracle, the gloom and the despair, culminating in the awful phenomenon of possession at the time of our Blessed Lord's appearance on the earth, all bear testimony to an adverse occupancy of humanity by one who was known as the "Prince of this World."

Or, look again at the Demon-worship, in African systems, with its religion of fear and dread, where all love of a Father God has passed into servile fear of some cruel tyrant who has to be appeased and coaxed, lest he strike, without a word, the votary who has unwittingly displeased him.

It is not a little remarkable, if we can credit what has lately appeared in our daily papers, that, out of the turbulence and atheism and immorality of the day, a society has appeared in Paris, international in its character, of the Luciferans, whose object is to set up Lucifer as the acknowledged God of the world. Already two temples have been dedicated to Satan in Paris, and there is a sect of Devil-worshippers, with their motto "Voluptas Peccati."[1]

It seems, at least, reasonable to imagine that some of the phenomena of so-called spiritualism and the like, in which many, who have lost faith in God yet bring themselves to believe, have, at least, a substratum to justify the name.

[1] See *Daily Chronicle*, April 20, 1894; *St. James's Gazette*, April 20, 1894.

It would not be hard to make out a case against those who deny the reality of possession in our Blessed Lord's time, showing that something very like possession may be found now.

And if we look around us in the world to-day, there, it is plainly to be seen, is the same unaltering plan of attack. There stands the sovereign will within man, plied with suggestion and besieged with importunity; there is the attack delivered with consummate skill, where fear has crumbled in the rampart, or desire has loosened the barrier which separates from evil.

"If thou let this man go, thou art not Cæsar's friend."[1] This is a tender place in the side of a man who has to keep well with the government; and first there is perturbation, and then there is vacillation, and then there is protest, and then comes the crash.

"Art not thou also one of His disciples?"[2] is a delicate thrust in the unprotected region of one who has taken in more ground than he can defend; and he topples over before the blow. Here thirty pieces of silver are catching Judas;

[1] St. John xix. 12.   [2] St. John xviii. 25.

the desire of having is the ruin of Ananias and Sapphira.

There it is all around us to-day. First, the suggestion of evil, delivered in the weak place of defence; then the breaking down of the opposition by menace or allurement; then the consent of the will, on which depends victory. When this gives in, temptation has ripened into sin over the prostrate will, and whether the victory be carried further or not, as regards its sinfulness or the contrary, it is only a question of degree.

(2.) But as we have done in investigating previous questions, let us do also in this—let us interrogate the highest form of spiritual experience, and ask him who is trying to lead a spiritual life, whether he is conscious of dealing with a person, and whether the phenomena of temptation which he experiences correspond to that which Holy Scripture leads us to expect.

And it is no unimportant question which it does not concern us to decide—whether the attack is delivered by a person, or is merely the outcome of the workings of a principle.

If it be merely a principle which we have to deal with, we feel ourselves, to a certain extent, powerless under the working out of fixed laws, and we may easily fall into the new fatalism, which folds its hands before heredity and environment, and says, "I cannot help myself; blame my ancestors, not me. I have ceased to struggle. Improve my environment—it is the fault of society, not of me. Improve my surroundings by coercive legislation, and my temptations will cease."

But if we are dealing with a person, however much he may be removed from us in power or differ from us in condition, we have, at least, some ground of experience to guide us. We are dealing with an intelligence; we are dealing with a will: "he possesses, we believe, the very properties which are the essence of our manhood, only on a much larger scale than we." The same resolution which has helped us before now in dealing with an evil companion, and with the low tone of life around us, helps us still in dealing with an intelligence.

Subtle tactics are something which we can measure and grasp, not an impalpable principle, whatever that may mean, which has neither soul nor body, to be weighed, compressed, and overcome. And in interrogating the highest lives, we are struck at the outset with this difficulty: Why should good men be tempted at all? If by doing virtuous things we become virtuous, why is it that the good man has not elevated himself by habits of good, not only out of evil actions, but out of any connection with them by desire, or susceptibility, or otherwise?

It is a phenomenon difficult to explain on any hypothesis but one—that holy men should be tempted by evil thoughts and evil suggestions, that they never should be able to feel themselves safe. We have an extreme example of it, in the case of our Blessed Lord, Who, being incapable of sin, unless we suppose a contradiction which is impossible, was yet, if we are to believe Holy Scripture, once in a deliberate way, and afterwards in another form, subjected to temptation to evil; and although it is quite true that in His case temptation was purely external, without any sinful principle from within to meet it, and although it is also true that the more a man becomes like Christ, the more to him will temptation become external also, still the fact of His being tempted at all, points to an outside agent, who looks upon a good life as a personal insult to himself, and the practice of virtue as a revolt against the authority which he wishes to set up.

And once more, those who are striving to serve God will tell us, that they are most conscious, even more so than one who follows his appetites without a struggle, of a power, fierce, malignant, and desperately cunning, in whose hands opportunity and seduction are as skilfully manipulated as in the pages of *Faust* or *Macbeth*. They will tell us that they do not catch a sin as you catch a fever, from poisonous germs floating in the air, but that weakness and opportunity are skilfully manipulated and marvellously adjusted, so that they can confidently endorse as true to everyday experience the saying of the apostle, " We wrestle not against flesh and blood, but against principalities, against powers, against the rulers of the darkness of this world, against spiritual wickedness in high places."[1]

[1] Eph. vi. 12.

III.

It is worth while to interrogate this spiritual experience even closer.

Holy Scripture, as we know, lights up jets of Revelation in significant names and titles. It is so in the names of God, which are brilliant points of dazzling light, in which Revelation declares itself. In the same way, the titles and description of the powers of evil are minute and significant; they burn with a warning light over the dangerous reefs, where death lies hidden.

Of course, if the stream of Revelation, of which Israel was the recipient, is only a flood-water running off the submerged foundations of other and past religions, carrying on its surface strange and fantastic relics, which mingle with true and deeper realities, it is of little use to study them for more than general effect.

If the idea of Satan is derived from the remains of "Nature religion," or "the uncanny ghosts of Chaldea and Assyria," or is due to the influence of

Persian dualism,[1] it is of very little use to investigate the conception as based on experimental reality. But if, on the other hand, we believe that nothing, not even a name, is insignificant in Holy Scripture, it would be interesting, if nothing else, to ask the spiritual man, whether he has been able to detect any appropriateness in the familiar titles for the power of evil; whether we should catalogue them and analyze them as part of the interesting folk-lore of nations, or whether they have a basis in spiritual phenomena, to be seen and registered to this day on the wind-swept heights of the spiritual life.

(1.) For instance, what appropriateness is there in such a term as "Devil," the calumniator, the accuser? Is this the most prevailing and prominent characteristic of the Tempter, that he should be so described?

A man, strong in spiritual experience, will, if I mistake not, unhesitatingly answer "Yes." Who are the people in our everyday experience among the moving throngs of living souls, who, on the

[1] Schultz, "Old Testament Theology," vol. ii., p. 279 (Clark).

whole, do most harm, whose influence sweeps like a withering blast over the tender flowers of opening youth; in whose presence virtue finds it difficult to live, and seriousness to breathe; where we find the only way to escape is to break the glass of custom and convention, and let in anyhow and anywhere the breath of Heaven, that we may live? Are they not those who blight with cynicism, and just stab with sarcasm, and damn with doubt? A faint praise, a mild disparagement, a shrug of the shoulders will do it—our ideal is shattered.

"The missionaries with their wives and comfortable houses—excellent men, no doubt, but you know what the ordinary European thinks of them!"

"Dear old Adam and Eve, and Abraham and Job—charming stories! what a pity the critics and the students of comparative religions did not leave us alone!"

A turn of the voice will accentuate such a word as "pious" into an epithet from which we shrink. A ripple of sarcasm, even when its wave has subsided, leaves its marks on the tender surface of the soul.

Ah, we see, the spiritual man is right. There is nothing he so much dreads as this light disparagement which makes holiness ridiculous and serious thoughts difficult, which makes him doubt his own disinterestedness and takes the sunlight out of religion.

We see the Devil linking hands with political precepts, which say that "every man has his price;" with moral estimates, which say "no man will do any good except it be for his own interest to do so;" with an intellectual scepticism which resents the thought that human nature is a spoiled child, which can only be coaxed into being good by the promise of heaven, or goaded into it by the fear of hell.

The power of evil we see from the spiritual height is accurately described in that term which clothes him as a Devil. There it is; it does not come from Babylon or Persia, but it comes straight from human experience. There it is!—that monstrous form of fascinating beauty curled round the code of morality to sap the grounds of obedience, and bring in, under every seduction of art and beauty, the deadly poison which will vitiate vitality, as God's threats are emptied of their meaning, and men swallow poison, gaily re-echoing "Thou shalt not surely die." Who has brought us an exultation which means death, and a glory which means nakedness? Who has daubed his unattractive drab over prosaic duty, and covered rottenness and evil with spangles and paint? Who but an evil being who slanders God, and saps the glory, in the true, the beautiful, and the good.

We shall have to consider remorse at another time, one of the darkest shadows of the human heart. But the greatest saint knows, and knows to his cost, that he meets day by day a resistance which can best be described as coming from an accusing Devil. Who has not known what it is to have broken resolutions, and brushed past promises, and as he gazes at the littered heaps of duties left undone, and evil done instead of good, to feel the misery of the evil taunt, which impels to a further decline still? "To have fallen thus far suggests that the struggle is useless, and a lower platform desirable. Resolutions are bad things, they are only made to be broken; and the splinters of broken rules, pierced by the shock of the world, suggest that a free and unarmoured life is the best. To curb the horse of passion too tight is to make it rear and become restive;" and so he leads on, where he does not fear to declare his full purpose, to that final manifestation of his nature when he says, "There are some things in every one's life which he cannot master; give up the foolish belief in an 'Omnipotent God.' 'If thou, therefore, wilt worship me, all shall be thine.'[1]"

There are clouds which sweep across the mountain which the spiritual man has accurately analyzed, and he tells us they are all to be properly described as of the Devil—the accuser. Scruples, for instance, in which simulated defeats are made to do duty for real ones, in pulling a man down—or the craving for assurance, or for happiness, often one of the worst spiritual signs, which waits on selfish and presumptuous courses. When a man thinks himself safe because he feels

[1] St. Luke iv. 7.

no pain, and, like a boy whistling in the dark to reassure himself, calls out loudly, "I am so happy." Melancholy, again, depression, fretfulness —let the spiritual man analyze them for us, and he will say they all come from the accuser, as he knew who wrote, "Fret not thyself, else shalt thou be moved to do evil." [1]

(2.) An equally powerful revelation, as the spiritual man will tell us, is the word "Satan" —the adversary; he who opposes us, who steps before us when we come forth to serve God, and paints for us the glorious landscape of world-power, the satisfaction of ambition, the gratification of desire, and promises all, at the price of one sin or a taint in our allegiance.

It is Satan who stands before the devoted life which has emptied itself, and has taken the resolution and made the choice, and determined to embrace the cross, and says, "Be it far from thee: this shall not be unto thee." [2]

He gets behind the seductive affection of friends, the soft pleading of our own will. He suggests what

[1] Ps. xxxvii. 8. [2] St. Matt. xvi. 22.

he calls higher duties and more obvious spheres of usefulness; if we will consecrate our powers to God, at least we shall keep back part of the price.

It is Satan who stands at the entrance gate of all vocation, stopping the rich young ruler from his great call, driving away the half-formed longing for a higher life, as he murmurs, "Have any of the rulers or of the Pharisees believed on Him?"[1]

He hangs round the difficult steps which mark the approach to goodness, the preparation for the sacraments, the shame of repentance, the difficulty of prayer, the simplicity of the Bible, the strictness of Christianity.

We find it almost impossible, until the enemy stands unmasked as Satan, to understand the extreme difficulty of the simplest forms of good. But it becomes easier to realize, and prepares us for the fierceness of the struggle, as the spiritual man shows us Satan—no uncanny ghost of Persian superstition, but a real adversary, the weight of whose resistance must be measured, and allowed for, in any effort after goodness.

[1] St. John vii. 48.

(3.) A whole bundle of titles yet remain, which we cannot stop to examine—picturesque, suggestive, and significant. Yet do not let us minimize our Blessed Lord's startling statement, which experience, the highest experience, confirms every day, "He was a murderer from the beginning."

The evil being who tempts us is a being of extreme malignity, and his assaults end in death. We can trace it all through history; we can trace it in that saddest of all experiences—the fall of good men. Satan's mission is to kill. It is a conflict in which no quarter is given. Look at Samson, Saul, Solomon, Judas. Look at the scars of good men, and you will see how experience does but once more confirm Revelation, when it shows us that we fight with a foe who deals in poisoned weapons. Whatever else it may be, this subject can never be unimportant or unpractical. And we may fairly say, it is a subject which spiritual men ought to decide.

It is quite possible that those who have never fought any harder battle than the ordinary vital

[1] St. John viii. 44.

battles of morality, are practically unconscious of many of the deeper phenomena of evil, which a spiritual man cannot ignore.

A mathematician is not qualified by his mathematics to study music, nor a chemist by his studies to analyze art. In like manner, the highest intellectual equipment does not qualify a man for spiritual experience, and we could not make a greater mistake than to submit delicate and complex facts of temptation to those who, by the very nature of the case, are unqualified judges.

LECTURE VI.

THE PHENOMENA OF THE PUNISHMENT OF SIN.

"The wrath of God is revealed from heaven against all ungodliness and unrighteousness of men, who hold the truth in unrighteousness."—ROM. i. 18.

FROM first to last in Holy Scripture the revelation of God's wrath against sin is of such a character as to make us wonder whether we have really any adequate conception of what sin is which is punished, or of God Who punishes.

I.

(1.) In the opening pages of the Bible a trifling act of disobedience, as we are tempted to call it, involves all the world, innocent and guilty alike, in the severe consequences which follow a serious sin—death and suffering and a general break up of man's relations with God.

In the New Testament we are perplexed and

startled with the measured accents in which punishment which is everlasting is spoken of: of soul and body both being destroyed in hell;[1] of outer darkness, with weeping and gnashing of teeth;[2] of the possibility of a man's losing his own soul;[3] of everlasting punishment as the alternative to everlasting life;[4] of an undying worm,[5] and an undying fire; of Judas the Apostle being in such a desperate state, that it were good for him never to have been born;[6] of a resurrection of damnation, as well as a resurrection of life;[7] of an eternal sin;[8] of a sin for which no forgiveness is possible;[9] thus linking on the unknown and untried life with the awful phenomena of God's wrath on sin in history and experience, which lies with blighting, withering effect across uprooted cities and dismembered empires, which exhibits champions of God turned into dishonoured slaves, inspired saints into trembling criminals, and lingering taint and slowly working curse, dread, inevitable, inexorable.

[1] St. Matt. x. 28. [2] St. Matt. viii. 12.
[3] St. Matt. xvi. 26. [4] St. Matt. xxv. 46.
[5] St. Mark ix. 44. [6] St. Mark xiv. 21.
[7] St. John v. 29. [8] St. Mark iii. 29. [9] St. Matt. xii. 32.

Wherever we turn, sin is like some dreadful spiritual explosive, whose effects are out of all proportion to its size and apparent importance.

If Holy Scripture is a revelation of the purpose and mercy of God, it is equally a revelation of God's wrath on sin.

It begins with the exhibition of a curse destined to work itself out, until the winding up of the ages. It ends by speaking of another state, in which the extreme malignity of sin meets with a punishment which we cannot understand, while we shrink from any definite realization of it.

Our Blessed Lord was once asked in view of these awful statements, "Lord, are there few that be saved?"[1] and we know how He gave no direct answer, but an answer which amounted to this: Act in your daily life as if the saved were only few. Strive and labour, and remember the narrow gate and the fallacy of majorities.

I think we may say that, however we may analyze and explain our Blessed Lord's words, whatever comfort we may get out of the meaning

[1] St. Luke xiii. 23.

of the words αἰώνιος and κόλασις, however we may shrink from their full meaning, still the impression He meant to leave on men's hearts was, that sin was of such a deadly nature that, if persisted in and not forgiven, it would be punished for ever in a future state, with punishments only inadequately to be described in human language.

> "Christ on Himself, considerate Master, took
> The utterance of that doctrine's fearful sound;
> The Fount of Love, His servants sent to tell
> Love's deeds, Himself revealed the sinner's hell."

(2.) We know the controversy which has sprung up, even in our own days, as to the final punishment of the wicked, and as to what Holy Scripture really does say about it.

There are many who deny, and indignantly deny, that Holy Scripture sets forth, or that the Church represents it as setting forth, a theory of punishment for sin, which they assert is derogatory to the nature of God, degrading to man, and damaging to the true interests of morality. God is love, and God is just; human nature is not to be driven into right-doing, and that by threats which violate all proportion and degrade all sense of sonship and self-respect.

It is necessary just to glance, if we do nothing else, at the principal mitigations which have been advanced of a theory of punishment so difficult and so severe, by men anxious to apologize for God, and to soften the terrible outlines of vengeance, admittedly difficult to understand or to defend.

And so accordingly we are met, first, by the Universalists, who say that we must explain the less intelligible passages of Holy Scripture by the more intelligible, and not suppose it possible that God can deny Himself or ever have said anything which would stultify His justice, love, and mercy. All will in some way be saved. "As in Adam all die, even so in Christ shall all be made alive."[1]

Others again tell us, if I rightly understand their contention, that sin will be ultimately eradicated, and that punishment will of necessity go with it. But that for all that, the penalty of past

---

[1] 1 Cor. xv. 22. See on this passage "The Resurrection of the Dead," Milligan, in loc.

sin will linger on in a form of eternal punishment, just as a man may survive, doomed all his life to be maimed in the loss of an arm or leg, a memorial of a past accident.

Others, again, tell us that eternal life is only for the good, that immortality is conditional on goodness, and that all the fierce denunciation poured on sin points to the extermination of the sinner, as unworthy of life, not to his lingering in eternal torment.

All these explanations bear witness to the main point for which we are now contending, that Holy Scripture represents the punishment on sin as so tremendous, that men find a difficulty in accepting it, and must either deny it altogether or explain it away.

Here once more we should do well to ask ourselves, are we quite sure that we have any conception of what sin really is?

(3.) If we would attempt to measure it at all, we must take our stand on Calvary and gaze on the cross. Why was this tremendous act necessary? Why was it, in the nature of things, of obligation, that an event should take place which human language can hardly set forth without a contradiction and an absurdity,—that God should die?[1]

Is sin such a thing that God cannot wipe it out by an act of His omnipotent will? Is sin such a tremendous thing, that man, who can bring it on, cannot yet take it off, that it necessitated the great renunciation of Divine glory, the emptying out of the royal prerogatives, and the humiliation of the Incarnation?

The difficulty which surrounds the punishment of the wicked is a difficulty which is best measured by the mystery of the Atonement, in which sin reached its head, and suffered its most awful punishment.

II.

If we now turn to examine experience, such experience as every one has access to, we ask ourselves at once—

---

[1] Such a condensed statement the author believes to be defensible, on the analogy of Acts xx. 28.

Is the punishment on sin which goes on all around us, whose facts none can deny, any more explicable, I had almost said defensible, than the punishment on sin which is proclaimed as awaiting men in another world?

Suppose, for one moment, a human being, gazing out on this world as yet uncreated by Almighty God, or as yet unformed for human habitation; and suppose him to meditate on the constitution and condition of such a world about to be started, having an All-wise and All-loving Being as its Creator.

Of course he would say, as God is All-wise, the world which He is about to create will be a world in which evil will find no place. No one will be allowed to lose his peace of mind by doing anything which God hates.

What do we find in actual experience?

A world created by God in which the All-wise has allowed evil to run riot, to the detriment of man's peace and the perpetual bewilderment of his understanding.

Still looking out on the unformed world, an

observer would say, a world created by a loving God will have no taint of possible fatalism or dead-weighted heredity. Every man will be punished for his own misdeeds, and rewarded for his own virtues. We shall not find good defeated and evil triumphant, or innocent children suffering for the misdeeds of the father.

What, as a matter of fact, do we find? Children weighted from their birth with the dower of a curse; evil inclinations, evil surroundings, pulling them down. Some who, speaking lightly, we say have not got a chance, who breathe in evil with the atmosphere in which they are born, and suck in corruption with their mother's milk, tortured in body, stunted in soul, blinded in moral apprehension for no fault of their own. Is God just? men passionately cry.

How hopelessly adrift is our thoughtful friend, as he gazes out on a world to be created by God![1]

His ideas of justice, mercy, and love, all receive shocks as he comes to see the world existing in a way which he would have pronounced to be

[1] See Cook's Boston Lecture, "Love and Marriage," p. 150.

impossible. And as he walked through the world, again and again he would say, Is this punishment just, is it merciful?

Just one trifling deflection, a mistake even, and how punished! Saul exceeds his orders or falls short of them in the matter of Amalek; he is punished for rejecting God. David repents of a sin of overmastering temptation, but there is no withdrawing of the sword from his house. A man does but make a mistake; he cannot recover his place.

Is it commensurate, this fearful punishment on evil-doing—is it commensurate with the offence?[1] Is a sin of the appetite to be punished with loss of reason, with exquisite and refined nerve-tortures, with a lingering taint which reaches on to ages yet unborn?

Truly a man contemplating the punishment of sin here in this present state, so certain, so unrelenting, so adjusted to the offence, so everlasting as far as this world goes, working independently of repentance however heartfelt and accepted,

---

[1] See Cook's Boston Lecture, "Orthodoxy," p. 24.

would feel that, if he thinks it necessary to defend Almighty God, he must begin with the mysteries of experience here in this world, which are quite as difficult as any which he may be called upon to explain in view of the world to come. Wherever he turns he is met with the same phenomena—sin, a little sin, terribly punished, exhibiting a malignity which ordinary methods seem inadequate to reach.

The treatment of sin as exhibited, threatened, and enforced in Holy Scripture, cannot be discussed on *a priori* grounds. We are dealing with a mystery, which we can see everywhere, but explain never. Sin needed the Atonement. Sin wrung from our Blessed Lord some of the sternest words ever spoken by human lips. Sin alarms and puzzles still all who trace its terrible effects.

III.

Hitherto we have looked at human experience, as exhibiting the same problems, and needing the same apologies, in treating of the punishment of sin, as Holy Scripture.

Now let us look at some of the characteristics of that punishment, and see whether they correspond with the divine record of God's wrath.

And first of all, we are met with the permanence of punishment on sin, enshrined in such words as "everlasting," "where their worm dieth not," and the like.

It seems peculiarly useless to try and etymologically empty words of their meaning at this time of day, in the same breath in which we try to represent our Blessed Lord, with a kenosized knowledge, or else with a deliberate accommodation, adapting Himself to the standpoint of His hearers.

It is little use pointing out that a bank-note is made only of paper, if it has a currency, with those who use it, equivalent to valuable metal.

There can be no doubt that the general impression which our Blessed Lord's words conveyed was, that there were some sins for which the punishment was permanent. The best test of the difficulty experienced by those who try to prove the opposite, will be found in the shifts and expedients devised to explain the text, in which our Blessed Lord says of Judas, "Good were it for that man if he had never been born."[1]

Does experience bear out in any way this permanence of punishment following on sin? Surely in a very remarkable way. If we look into the strange and picturesque imagery of the nether world, as portrayed in the Greek and Latin poets, what a large part this persistence of punishment plays!

> "Sedet, æternumque sedebit,
> Infelix Theseus."[2]

Ixion for ever turns his wheel; Tantalus for ever seeks to satisfy his insatiable thirst.

Or look at the marvellous working out of Nemesis in the Greek tragedies, and the inevitable punishment of even involuntary defilement.

We have already alluded to a common experience in everyday life, where sin may have ceased but the punishment remains, and, as far as this world goes, is everlasting. Look at the victim of intemperance, who slowly and surely undermines his health. He wakes up to his condition, say at the

---

[1] St. Mark xiv. 21.   [2] Virgil, "Æneid," vi. 617.

age of forty; he turns to God, he repents, he is forgiven. Does he recover his health? He is punished to the end of the chapter, repentant though he be, and is chastised even while he is accepted.

Take a higher example still. Look at the strange love of the cross, of austerities, displayed by the saints of God, even where no passion remains to be subdued and no rebellious evil to be crushed.

Perhaps the strangest example of this that has ever been seen, is to be found in that wonderful episode in the life of St. Francis of Assisi, in which he is credited with having received the marks of the sacred stigmata, in union with the passion of our Blessed Lord. I quote from the recent Protestant life of that saint, appreciative yet critical, in which M. Sabatier says: "He [St. Francis] was consumed with the fever of saints, that need of immolation which wrung from St. Theresa the passionate cry, 'Either to suffer or to die.'"[1] We find traces of it again in a more modern divine, the Père Lacordaire, whose austerities and whose love of discipline

---

[1] Sabatier, "Life of St. Francis of Assisi," p. 293.

surprise us.[1] It is the same spirit which we find breathing through the ardent expression of St. Paul: "I am crucified with Christ, nevertheless I live:"[2] "Who . . . fill up that which is behind of the afflictions of Christ in my flesh for His body's sake, which is the Church."[3]

The sense of sin to be atoned for, to be corrected by lifelong suffering, meets us again and again in the biographies of holy men, and—may we also say it?—whether they wish it or not, struggle as they may, wrestle as they may, how awful it is that the old weakness remains as a punishment, where it has ceased to be a temptation! And the sense of guilt remains as a scourge, and the memory of sin as a perpetual penance.

The permanence of punishment on sin lingers around us in many strange indications and unlooked-for fashions, and seems to say that Holy Scripture utters a voice which is but the echo of our own conscience, when it speaks of everlasting punishment.

---

[1] See "Inner Life of Father Lacordaire," chap. xiv.
[2] Gal. ii. 20.   [3] Col. i. 24.

Another aspect of punishment on sin, which stands out before us, is its great severity.

All those mysterious expressions, such as "salted with fire," the "gnawing worm," the "unquenched flame," how terrible they are! If we could only see the poor actors in life's brutal show, who have been butchered by sin, and who are carried away to die! The world covers up their remains quickly, and a little clean sawdust makes it all easy to attract fresh victims. If we dared to lift the veil from only two sins, the punishments which follow would scare and appal us.

It is only by forgetting them and ignoring them and counting on the exception that does not come, that men can go on sinning.

But quite apart from this, ask the spiritual man, the man whose sins, it may be, have not been gross or wilful, what have been the most severe pains of his life. And he will tell you there is no unhappiness to compare with the unhappiness which follows on committed sin.

What a dark chapter in human life is that over which is written the one word "remorse!" What can it be that should have the power to make a man so utterly wretched, so despairing, which even rends his heart in twain and drags from him the agonized confession "I have sinned"? Why is it not sufficient for him to take a turn in the fresh air? to perform some act of amendment? to restore, to pay a voluntary fine? to take up a book and change the subject? to resolve never to offend in a like way again? It is no good. The inexorable cause will not be so appeased. There is a Person behind it all, a loving, tender form, which strikes with its mute appeal, and blames with its silent lips; which drives the sinner on and on, until remorse ripens into repentance and then pours forth, "Against Thee only have I sinned, and done this evil in Thy sight," or, alas! hardens into despair, until the love of God Himself seems to die away, and the sinner is left with a numbing care, which turns his heart into stone.[1] It is a startling witness to the malignity of sin, that its presence in the pure heart should have such power to scourge and torture.

[1] See, on Remorse, some striking remarks in Mr. Illingworth's "Bampton Lectures," 1st edition, pp. 17, 35.

When Charles IX. of France gave orders to kill Coligny, he is reported to have said, "Assassinate Admiral Coligny, but leave not a Huguenot in France to reproach me." We know something, all of us, of those virtues which stand round the committed sin and bitterly reproach us.

The sufferings of the hardened sinner are coarser and more terrible, when at last they make themselves felt on his deadened sensibility; but the suffering which sin inflicts—lesser sins, sins hardly known as sins to coarse minds—on the sensitive conscience of the servant of God, is a terrible witness to a dread possibility, which may take place, when God steps aside from the path of "an eternal sin" and lets it take its course.

Another set of terms, which speak of being "cast out," "shut out from the bridegroom's presence," as "being without," witnesses in unmistakable language to the punishment of sin as a loss. This aspect, indeed, is the most intelligible, and makes the least demands on human consciousness.

We all of us feel that there are certain golden blessings which sin takes with it, never to return.

Innocency itself, that priceless possession whose value we do not know until it is gone, can never return.[1] Penitence is very beautiful, but it is not innocence. That pure, unspotted soul which can see God, can never cease to lament, as a very expulsion from Eden, the clouding, deadening effect of admitted sin. And so loss goes hand-in-hand with sin all down the course of life; it is a game of chance from which no one ever yet has been known to rise up the winner.

The intellectual sin, ending in unbelief, "usually," we have been told, "due to indolence, often to prejudice, and never a thing to be proud of,"[2] leads to the loss out of life of some of its dearest and best treasures; and adds another fact to that generalization, that man without God is thoroughly miserable. This has been expressed to us with startling clearness quite recently. "Some men are not conscious of the cause of this misery: this, however, does not prevent the fact of their being

---

[1] See Mr. Illingworth, "University and Cathedral Sermons," No. 6.
[2] See "Thoughts on Religion" (Romanes), p. 145.

miserable. For the most part, they conceal the fact as well as possible from themselves by occupying their minds with society, sport, frivolity of all kinds, or, if intellectually disposed, with science, art, literature, business, etc. This, however, is but to fill the starving belly with husks. I know from experience the intellectual distraction of scientific research, philosophical speculation, and artistic pleasure: but am also aware that even when all are taken together and well sweetened to taste, in respect of consequent reputation, means, social position, etc., the whole concoction is but as high confectionery to a starving man. He may cheat himself for a time, especially if he be a strong man, into the belief that he is nourishing himself by denying his natural appetite, but soon finds he was made for some altogether different kind of food, even though of much less tastefulness, as far as the palate is concerned."[1]

And if intellectual sins spell loss, bodily sins no less run away with opportunities which never come back. Waste your youth, you have but one chance;

[1] "Thoughts on Religion" (Romanes), p. 151.

waste your health, you have but one chance; waste your opportunity, the same never comes again.

"O my God, make me what I might have been had I never sinned." It is the voice of one who saw what a grand thing life might be, and how much had come in with only a little sin.

It is in the region of spiritual experience, where we shall find the loss most emphasized. Where and to whatever extent sin has come in, there, and to that extent, is the loss of that peace which the soul so much covets, which has found union with God. Sometimes, without being conscious of any very grave fall, we feel at the same time we can only say of our spiritual life in the words of the General Confession, that "there is no health in us." We do not feel strongly the enthusiasm of good, we feel irritated and depressed by the presence of evil. We do not get on; when we have spent some time in mending the defects of the machinery, it snaps again, and life seems spent in repairs, rather than in useful progress.

In ordinary matters, when we determine to do a thing, we can for the most part carry it through, but here we fall back baffled at our own want of success, and our spiritual life becomes to us a burden and a despair, for it seems paved with good intentions.

The loss of peace in believing, which takes the word of God out of the Bible, and His presence from the sacrament, and His life from religion, tells us clearly what is meant by loss, as a punishment for sin, and how easily sin may be causing it, almost without our being aware of it.

What are known as the seven deadly sins, sins, that is, in grave matters forbidden under grave restrictions, are capable of pushing their tendrils into the most carefully guarded life, and are often allowed to strangle it before their presence is even suspected.

Irritability is not recognized as anger, nor liking to be comfortable as gluttony, nor rivalry as envy, nor evil thoughts as lust, nor indolence as sloth, nor saving propensities as avarice; and the soul becomes first aware of their presence by a sense of loss.

IV.

All agree in the punishment which follows sin, and yet, alas! sin still goes on.

On a subject so fearful, we must be careful not to venture outside what is written, nor to dogmatize where our Blessed Lord gave no direct answer. We need not puzzle about the future; we know at least the general impression which He gave us, and certainly, if we are wise, we shall act as if it were literally true.

But let us, if we can, explain the present; we need look no further than the horizon of this world to see mysteries equally puzzling, equally terrible. Sin enters the world, itself pregnant with death;[1] where it has once alighted, its presence can never be forgotten, even if its damage be condoned. It leaves its permanent scar, its smarting blow, and its sense of loss. Carry this on into a state where penitence has been rejected and forgiveness is unknown, and you have "the everlasting sin," where free-will has been respected and free-will has won

---

[1] " Ἡ δὲ ἁμαρτία ἀποτελεσθεῖσα ἀποκύει θάνατον," St. James i. 15.

its deadly way, and through punishment, pain, and loss, cries out, "We will not have this man to reign over us."

And yet punishment on sin is not all harm.

> "Minds which verily repent
> Are burdened with impunity
> And comforted by chastisement.
> That punishment's the best to bear
> That follows soonest on the sin;
> And guilt's a game where losers fare
> Better than those that seem to win."

There is a punishment on sin which is worse than all, and that is the penal answer to that dread prayer, "Let us alone!"

LECTURE VII.

THE PHENOMENA OF REDEMPTION.

"For as in Adam all die, even so in Christ shall all be made alive."—1 Cor. xv. 22.

HITHERTO our investigation of experience has led us through the gloomy region of sin, failure, and disappointment, where the faculties of man work with a strange tendency to error and deflection, under a bias which seems sometimes too much for them, in an environment which poisons and represses.

The history of the world seems a sad picture of unfulfilled hopes, of progress along a road littered with failure and strewn with disasters, where sin and punishment walk hand-in-hand, and mock at human resolution.

I.

And yet, if we study Revelation, we are conscious of another strain running through its records from first to last, correcting, revising, restoring, elevating, with an interpenetrating stream of mercy.

If Revelation is the history of the working out of what we know as the Fall, it is equally the history of the working out of Redemption.

And Holy Scripture shows us this power manifesting itself in particular ways, and by methods always uniform and consistent.

The world is not left to its failure and sin as a hopeless wreck, which must be allowed as speedily as possible to work out its misshapen course and accomplish its irretrievable doom. But Redemption follows close upon the ruined mechanism, and repairs it as far as possible, and fits it for new uses and fresh purposes. Redemption is not only in spite of the world's ruin, but also by means of the world's ruin, with the greatest economy of purpose and adherence to design. If God made the world for His glory, and man ruined it by his rebellion, God still tends to effect by Redemption His eternal purposes for which He created it.

So we may read the record of Revelation. Man, the reasonable centre round which all created things revolved, had to be restored into his proper relationship to his environment. There were certain well-ordered, clearly defined stages in this restoration.

First, there was the opening in the gloom which encompassed man about—the gloom of guilt; which took the form of a promise, and produced the birth of hope, and created the longing for an ideal, with a hope of reaching it, which became such a power in the world. The Seed of the woman was to bruise the head of the serpent.[1] In the Seed of the faithful patriarchs all the families of the earth should be blessed.[2] And man toiled and developed a higher pleasure than the pleasure of appetite, the honest joy of work, which redeemed the curse of toil; and men, still guided by this promise, left home and comforts[3] and ease in obedience to the call of God, and shaped their whole life in fulfilment of an ideal.

Men in this early stage redeemed themselves from the bondage of sense by following the guidance of a promise.

[1] Gen. iii. 15.   [2] Gen. xxii. 18.   [3] See Heb. xi.

Another stage was the development of the powers, and the reconstruction of the will, which had been weakened by sin.

Man passed away from the childhood stage, where his one virtue was obedience, which kept him straight, so long as he followed the guidance of the eye of God, into the region of law, where "Thou shalt not" and "Thou shalt" developed a system of morality, by which he could walk alone, hedged round by rule, beneath the tempting trees of desire, which still grew round the road of life.[1]

The power to be good was being developed in the world, and then, when the tree of life seemed almost bare, and the winds of passion had swept away the greatness of the peculiar people, and laid low the highest intellectual development of the world; when the empire of law and order was, in turn, beginning to totter, then appeared that one fair

[1] The author is quite unable to accept the modern theories, which, instead of the usual "Law and the Prophets," bid us speak of "the Prophets and the Law," which arrangement, apart from all other questions, in the words of the late Dr. Liddon, deposes the Law from its chronological and authoritative place, and, as it would seem to the author, subverts the whole history of the moral and religious education of the world.

fruit of the tree of life, of whom was born Jesus the Son of God—God in man, using human nature, human powers, human knowledge, human conditions, human temptations, human suffering. And then, when men saw God thus using human nature, and working with it in our flesh, it witnessed the achievements of goodness. Humanity became heir to that great deposit of example, looking at which, in all our difficulties we may ask, and not ask in vain—what would Jesus Christ have done?

The Redemption did not stop here. Holy Scripture, if it tells us anything, speaks of two achievements, which far surpass any mere force of example—the one is the Atonement, effected by the death of Christ upon the cross, the other is "the extension of the Incarnation"[1] in the sacraments and the Church, whereby Christ becomes the new life, as well as the example of His people.

Such, in the briefest outline, is the history of Redemption, which is so prominent in the pages of the Bible, on every stage of which treatises have

[1] For this phrase see Jeremy Taylor, "Worthy Communicant," i. 2.

been written and human thought has exercised itself to the utmost.

But, true to our method, let us proceed to ask ourselves, what traces do we find of this redemptive strain in human nature around us to-day? In man, who so faithfully reflects the catastrophe of the Fall, are there to be found also traces of Redemption? Has anything been done for the perverted environment, or, at least, for man's relationship to it?

In the short time that remains to us, we can but touch on the fringe of this subject, but we can see that "where sin abounded, grace did much more abound."[1]

II.

And, first of all, we are met by this fact, which we notice also in Revelation, that redemption from sin takes place in spite of, and even by means of the world.

We read in inspired history of the singular fate and deliverance which once overtook the Jews;

[1] Rom. v. 20.

how, when the decree had gone forth for their massacre and extirpation, Esther obtained a reversal, but only to this extent—inasmuch as the laws of the Medes and Persians alter not, the original decree could not be abolished, but the Jews, by her intervention, obtained the right to defend themselves, and so arrested their extermination.

This is a parable of what Christ has procured for His people. The environment in which men live, can never, as we have seen, be made thoroughly healthy and good; it will always continue to be "the World." " Advancing civilization, in so far as the advance of civilization means increase of knowledge, of culture, and of wealth, does not itself lead to moral development, but, on the contrary, brings with it in its train a host of new and formerly unknown evils and temptations ; with the advance of knowledge, old ideas and old associations lose their hold upon the mind of men, while various and attractive forms of vice become familiar to them."[1]

[1] "Christ in the World," Foley, Donnellan Lectures, p. 109.

A law more stringent than the law of the Medes and Persians has passed its decree of cause and effect upon this world. It always must remain an unhealthy place, and the only possible improvement which can happen to environment is to improve man, so that he may improve his own environment, and make proper use of it when thus improved. And so it has been, and is, one of the distinctive features of Christianity, that it takes the world as it finds it, and improves it and extracts blessing out of its very curses.

Take, for instance, the phenomenon of pain. Christianity neither ignores it, nor despises it, nor is it afraid of it, but uses it, and out of it extracts a host of solid virtues. Or take temptation, again. We are often told that the indifferent accommodation in the houses of our poorer neighbours makes virtue impossible; that hunger and want breed theft, by a natural law. Yet, alas! we know that a many-roomed house does not mean virtue, nor plenty of food and money exemption from some of the lowest forms of theft, such as running into debt without the means of paying.

Christ, out of the very fierceness of temptation, produces solid virtues, so that His inspired writer can say, " My brethren, count it all joy when ye fall into divers temptations; knowing this, that the trying of your faith worketh patience. But let patience have her perfect work, that ye may be perfect and entire, wanting nothing." [1]

Here, at the very outset, we have surely a confirmation of what Holy Scripture leads us to expect of a redemption which uses the broken failures of this fallen world, and not only uses them again, but extracts out of them fresh developments of good. In studying the experimental history of Redemption, we shall see triumphs over nature, in which grace not only gains a victory over evil, but actually re-adapts it to great uses. We shall notice triumphs over environment, so that we shall find it impossible to say, where Judas falls at the very side of Christ, and St. Matthew mounts the apostolic throne from the publican's counter, that a man is what circumstances make him, and is simply

[1] St. James i. 2, 3, 4.

held upright to do good, and crushed down to do evil.

Now, as we detected in Revelation three stages of redemptive working, so we shall find in human experience all around us a similar working of redemptive power.

Human nature being what it is, it is not a little remarkable to find the wish to be good so commonly displayed, at least where this wish has not been perverted or crushed out; a wish running from the half-felt desire to be better, and to do better, up to the craving for holiness, which asks of God, not His, but Himself.[1] Here we have that ideal, which answers in us to the promise of better things which cheered the patriarchs.

Of course, it may be asserted that the phenomenon is by no means universal, that many are contented to go on in sin, and live a life without God in the world, or any wish for Him. Still we may remember that atrophy of the spiritual sense, and atrophy of the moral faculty[2] are well-known

---

[1] See Canon Gore's "Bampton Lectures," p. 36.
[2] Canon Gore, *vide sup.*

forms of spiritual disease, while this desire is sufficiently common to justify us in using it as a witness to the working of redemptive power in man.

It is said that the greatest criminals are anxious that their children should not follow in their steps nor share their fate. Most sinners, at all events in the earlier stages of their decline, promise to themselves a time when they will do better and return to nobler things. Surely there is a divine restlessness in man, which gives him but little peace, while he sits among the swine, and impels him to seek his Father's home in penitence.

The promise of victory, the hope of better things —we all know what these are in our struggle with the Devil, the accuser, who objects to us the weight of our sin, the chains of habit, the crime of offended majesty, and how again and again we have been cheered by a promise of release, and have felt our powers, and realized our destiny, and have obtained deliverance, because we never lost the hope of it.

But take it in its highest development, in the scorn of the lower life, which impels the saint of

God to push ever further and further after his ideals of goodness.

First, the appetites are shown that nothing which they can bring can satisfy the soul; that if obedience was once broken by appetite, that appetite can now be perfectly curbed by obedience. To have safely passed the life of appetite is in itself by no means a barren victory; the very fierceness of the conflict has left behind it a strength of discipline, which stands the life in good stead for fiercer conflicts. Then there comes the view from the mountain of world-power and world-dominion; but still the ideal of goodness beckons higher, in a hunger and thirst after righteousness. A mere intellectual triumph will not satisfy, or a life based on this world; the power to trample down pride and ambition, the love of being unknown, the desire to be a servant, take their place: and surely these, as they are common incidents in the saintly life, are very remarkable phenomena; they show redemptive power at work in the most stubborn region of human life. They parallel, in everyday life, the father of the faithful going out from home and kindred, declaring plainly that he seeks a better country, that is an heavenly, and that the very powers which the Fall trained downwards, until they bound a man fast to this perishable world, are, in redemptive Hands turned upwards, until "as an anchor of the soul, both sure and steadfast,"[1] they lay hold on that which is within the veil, a hope eternal in the heavens.

This restless longing of the soul, which will not be bound down by things of earth, is a very gracious unloosing of the dominion of appetite. Whether it be only the dissatisfaction which sin and imperfection bring, or whether it be the definite craving for a lofty ideal, it shows that redemptive power is at work still in the region of the appetite and the region of choice, and that if man has fallen by his own wilfulness, there are powers at work to raise him out of the very dissatisfaction of his fall and the insatiable craving, which will not be stilled by created things until it finds its peace in God.

[1] Heb. vi. 19.

"'Show me Thy glory, gracious Lord!
'Tis Thee,' he cries, 'not Thine I seek.'
Nay, start not at so bold a word
From man, frail worm and weak:

"The spark of his first deathless fire
Yet buoys him up, and high above
The holiest creature, dares aspire
To the Creator's love.

"The eye in smiles may wander round,
Caught by earth's shadows as they fleet;
But for the soul no help is found,
Save Him who made it, meet.

"Spite of yourselves, ye witness this,
Who blindly self or sense adore;
Else wherefore, leaving your own bliss,
Still restless, ask ye more?"[1]

Besides the wish for God, which will not be repressed, which reaches forth after ideals as full of hope as the promise was to the fathers, we see again a second redemptive phenomenon, which takes, in human experience, the place occupied in Revelation by the law, and that is the power to be good. Evidently, the world being

[1] "Christian Year," Thirteenth Sunday after Trinity.

what it is, if the Christian is to remain in it and be rescued in it and in spite of it and even by it, he must be strengthened for his passage through it and his contact with it. Man fell by weakness; he is to be redeemed by an access of strength.

And the seat of government, whereby alone a firm and equable rule can be maintained over an expanse of country exposed at every frontier to hostile incursions, is, we know, to be found in the will, which can be indefinitely strengthened or hopelessly degraded, which, even when most threatened and oppressed, can always count on all the reinforcements of redemptive love, "It is God which worketh in you both to will and to do;"[1] but which may be degraded to the obsequious service of the passions, or carried away by their mutinous onslaught, until it becomes, like the fatuous king whom Carlyle represents to us, shown on the balcony by torchlight, with a huge tricolour in his hat, to the mob which he had ceased to control, the semblance

[1] Phil. ii. 13.

of authority only adding to the degradation of surrender.

The sovereignty of the will is surely a matter which we should expect to find a subject of redemptive love, in giving a man that power over his actions which he finds so terribly impaired by centuries of inherited weakness.

Pause for one moment to consider the power of the will:—the very muscular and organic actions of the body wait for its word of command. One whose name is conspicuous in physical science, and who claims our respect in many other ways, has told us how that, after listening to a piece of music swiftly played by a brilliant executant, he calculated that, on an average, twenty-four notes were played in each second; that each of these required at least three distinct and voluntary movements of the muscles, and that each of these movements was directed by the will to a certain place with a certain force and a certain speed at a certain time, and each touch was maintained for a certain length of time. That thus there were, as we may say, five distinct and designed qualities in each of the seventy-two movements in each second,[1] and more besides in the region of sensation—he may truly say, "It is impossible to imagine what goes on in a brain thus employed."

It is the will which has to decide on the use to which it shall apply all the raw material of life, to decide whether the material shall lapse through lawlessness into evil, or be worked by discipline into good.

It is the will which meets desire, the rational desire for good, and, casting about for the means of its attainment through deliberation, selects one of those means in preference by deliberate choice.

It is the will which "selects and appropriates to itself, or exerts its influence upon the various material supplied by reason and desire,"[2] and so contributes to the formation of character—so mighty is the will, "the last appetite in deliberation."[3]

---

[1] Sir James Paget, see "Aspects of Modern Study," pp. 99, 100.
[2] Mr. Illingworth, "Bampton Lectures," chap. ii., p. 39.
[3] Hobbes, quoted in Mr. Illingworth's "Bampton Lectures,' chap. ii., p. 35; see also chap. ii. passim.

And any one who is trying in any way to control his actions and regulate his life, knows how impossible it is to drift, trusting to the current of life to take him right; daily and hourly he must decide, *i.e.* deliberately use his will, and this in little as well as great things.

We cannot keep the will as a magistrate to read the Riot Act, when things have proceeded to extremities; we cannot allow life to go on unchecked within us, as it were, managed by irresponsible agents. In great things and in little the will must act.

And redemptive power sets itself, as a fact of common experience, to brace the will. And this in a well-defined, carefully observed method.

God, while recognizing the power, has also always respected the freedom of the will; there is no compulsion, no forcing to choose one course, no driving into heaven, no extirpation of enemies by main force; each step in the conquest of life has to be won by man for himself, acting with God: using those methods which He has devised for our help.

No part of our being is to be suppressed and made inactive. There must be no aiming at a stolid insensibility to circumstances, in the midst of the pains and pleasures of life. God knows nothing of a suppression of the body, or a blind submission to a higher authority, or a placing of one's self in an artificial environment. The Christian has instead, while maintaining each part of his composite being complete and entire, to bring them each and all in their full working order under the power of the will, with the ultimate aim of bringing into captivity every thought to the obedience of Christ. And all this needs and is effected by grace of a very special kind.

We shall see in the next lecture how Christ has put human nature, as it were, in a consecrated precinct, wherein grace, as it is called, exercises a full and transforming power. "Go ye therefore," He said to His Church, "and make disciples of all the nations, baptizing them into the Name of the Father and of the Son and of the Holy Ghost: teaching them to observe all things whatsoever I commanded you: and lo, I am with you alway, even unto the end of the world." [1]

This is redemptive power, working in our midst, which enables a man to lift himself up from the dust.

How again and again we see it, strength coming through this environment, this spiritual precinct, which hedges a man round, not with the bristling hedge of a law, but with the loving support of enfolding grace! Look at St. Augustine, forsaking his sins and waxing vigorous and strong in the Lord! Look at men and women leading captive their lusts whose captives they were: the intemperate, sober; the sensual, chaste; the violent, self-contained; the niggard, bountiful; the coward, brave!

The transforming power of Christ, this strengthening of the will until it rules once more over its lawful domains! Who is there who does not know at least one example of this redemptive power? And if for all this we look askance at sacraments and sin apparently existing side by side, of prayer powerless to obtain and grace powerless to alter,

[1] St. Matt. xxviii. 19 (Revised Version).

let us remember this once more, that with God there is no mechanical religion, that everything has to be accepted by the will—even grace itself and the great powers of religion, by a very decided act of the will.

It is no easy matter to co-operate with God. It will not carry us far to sit down and say, "I am now, thank God, in the true Church, and therefore all will be well." Privilege, without the effort which privilege implies, if we have read the history of God's dealing with men at all carefully, is utterly useless. If we are in the true Church, and are deceitful, or not living the highest life, it profits us nothing. If we find the will still weak, in the full flow of grace, and sins still triumphant, and parts of our being under robber usurpation, do not let us blame God, but self which does not co-operate with God.

The will strengthened by redemptive grace is a phenomenon of daily experience, wherein Christ says "thou mayest" and "thou canst" do good; while the law said simply "thou shalt not do evil."

In the face of life's fiercest foes and its most

crying evils, we have a power in the strengthened will, which nothing can withstand.

And lastly, human experience bears this further witness also: not only is there the wish to be good, the craving for a high ideal, and the power to be good, in the marvellous strength of will, where we should hardly have expected to find it, but there are the striking examples of goodness, which take the place in our own experience which the life of the Incarnate God occupies in the history of the world.

The beauty of the Christian type of character is a standing witness to the power of redemptive love.

And we may notice at the outset that this character, so strikingly beautiful, is not the product of any one set of conditions.

It has been suggestively noticed that as there are flowers everywhere—even in cold Iceland, by the sea-marsh, on the roof, in the ditch, in the prison, in the rough wastes cleared here in London—so there are saints everywhere[1]—saints in Cæsar's household, a saint beneath the rough exterior of a

---

[1] Mr. Baring Gould, "Sermons to Children," No. xvii.

runaway slave, saints in the army, saints on shipboard, saints in the foul dens of this metropolis, saints among the enervating influence of its gilded pleasures.

There is such a thing, as we have already seen, as holiness, in spite of, yes, by means of, stern and unpromising surroundings. And we must also remember, if any would attribute this to character and not to Christianity—if any, that is, will say we can find you as good and self-denying men among the unbaptized and the unbelieving, among those who are conscientiously opposed to Christianity—that in forming an estimate of this kind we must take the best of each class, and not compare a careless Christian, or a Christian only strong in natural virtues, with an unbeliever who has lived conscientiously up to his lights and acted up to his convictions; we must take the best of each, in our comparison, and then see if any type of character has been produced which can compare with the Christian types.

Not only on the coercive side of character, as it were, must we look. We assume, as a matter of course, inward as well as outward purity, temperance, self-control, justice, fortitude, and the like,—but it is in those refinements which Christianity has produced, that we see the wonderful, transforming power of Redemption.

Consider, for instance, such a virtue as Love, which, in utter unselfishness and freedom from private gratification, gives out of self to God and man, which loses self in others and in doing good, which has ceased to feel the bit and bridle of rule, which is guided by the eye of God.

Or, look at Joy, again! What joy was there about those dejected figures turning their backs on ruined hopes? What joy is there about the sinner toiling after pleasure until he dies, or the selfishness of life which drains the cup of good things forgetful of others? There it is, that wonderful note of the Gospel, the sign of the smooth even working of the readjusted machine once torn asunder by sin, now reunited by God.

Look at Peace, again! That "tranquillity of order," that peace which passes all understanding, which keeps the heart and mind as with a garrison, through Jesus Christ. "Preaching peace through Jesus Christ" is the motto of the Christian wherever he goes, as the indwelling Spirit once more broods over chaos and, making His habitation in man, produces the true development of his character. Long-suffering, no less, which stands the Christian in such good stead, amidst cruel disappointments within and without. Gentleness, which proclaims the royal race, a nature not of this world. Goodness, which sheds beneficence all around its path. Faith, which trusts in God amid all the contradictions of the way. Meekness, which extracts by its paradoxical force the homage of a world which only believes in self-assertion. Temperance, which knows how to use aright all the manifold ingredients of life, with its contradictions and its enticements, its bitter and its sweet.

It may be that we rarely see this character; it may be we are put off by counterfeits: but there is no mistaking it when we do see it. Man, redeemed by Jesus Christ, makes it possible to realize the saying, that God created man in His own image; while it throws a light on the dogma of our Christian faith, that the Son of God, for us men and for our salvation, came down from heaven and was made man.

So the phenomena of life once more bear witness to the real existence of a power of redemption working in this fallen world.

Man wishes to rise above himself, man can rise above himself, and has succeeded in doing so.

"As in Adam all die, even so in Christ"—those who are in Christ, those who can claim that incorporation—"shall all be made alive."

[1] See, on this passage, "The Resurrection of the Dead" (Milligan), chap. iii.

LECTURE VIII.

THE PHENOMENA OF THE ATONEMENT AND GRACE.

"But thanks be to God, which giveth us the victory through our Lord Jesus Christ."—1 Cor. xv. 57.

This strain of Redemption, which we traced last time, as a dominant theme in the records of Revelation, will be found on closer examination to find its most intense expression in two great motives, whose presence we have before noticed without attempting to look into them more minutely, viz. the Atonement, as a mighty fact, which has readjusted the relationship of the universe to God, and Grace, which conveys the benefits won by that act to the individual soul, which is willing to receive it.

I.

The most superficial glance at the sacred Scriptures will show the prominent position assigned to the Atonement.

(1.) In the very forefront of the manifestation of the purposes of God, there stands the possibility of atonement. "The Lamb without blemish and without spot" was not only foreknown, but, as is also revealed to us, was, in the full language of the Apostle, slain from the foundation of the world.[1] Without attempting to discuss a question which must always remain insoluble, as to whether, had there been no necessity for an Atonement, there would still have been a Divine Incarnation; here, at all events, according to Holy Scripture, the possibility is provided for. The Lamb for the burnt offering is prepared.

We go on to trace this idea of the Atonement in the early mention of sacrifice, which found its full expression in the legalized and systematized sacrifices of the Law, with its rationale of atonement impressed on every offering, a rationale set forth by the author of the Epistle to the Hebrews in these words, "Without shedding of blood there is no remission."[2]

[1] See 1 St. Pet. i. 20; Rev. xiii. 8; Ellicott, "Salutary Doctrine," pp. 77, 78.
[2] Heb. ix. 22.

Under the Law, the giving of life to God for the averting of wrath has thus become firmly established, and yet, after all, it is the giving of a life which is not the offerer's own; the sin belonged to one living being, the pouring out of life to another.

Sin, as the sinner must have felt, at the best was not imputed, while it was yet not taken away. The impotence of the blood of bulls and goats to take away sin became more apparent, and the necessity for a sacrifice which should more truly be the offering of the sinner's self; and so through type and figure and prophecy we are led up to the cross, on which is exhibited the death of One who by His Incarnation represented the whole race of man: this is a point we must lay hold of; all the human race made reparation to God in Him.[1]

The whole human race could not meet together, like some vast congregation of penitents, and make reparation; but, nevertheless, it does make a real and all-sufficient reparation through this great

---

[1] Wordsworth, "The One Religion," p. 219.

Representative. All mankind suffers in Him, and yet, inasmuch as in every representation there must be a readiness on the part of an individual to undertake and submit to a larger share of the common responsibility than belonged to him individually, while we talk of expiation and ransom and redemption and rescue, we may still talk of substitution—not the substitution of the innocent for the guilty, in the sense that the guilty goes scot-free, but in the sense of the bearing of the brunt of the pain and sorrow which must fall on the Representative of all the world—on Him who alone could be the Representative of the world, as it ought to be in the eyes of God, because, in Himself sinless, He represented the ideal world; while in Himself taking up the sins of mankind, He represented the actual world.

Neither (even if the phrase be unscriptural, in the sense of not being the usual scriptural language in speaking of this mystery) need we altogether shrink from such an expression as that used in the second Article: "Christ reconciling the Father unto us."

There is what has been described as the "tension introduced by sin between the love and righteousness of God."[1]

Man has deprived his Creator of the perfection which He designed for him, by his sin and disobedience.[2] "He deprived God of everything which He had proposed to make out of human nature."[3]

And, indeed, we read of such expressions as the wrath of God abiding on unbelievers,[4] of the wrath of God being revealed from heaven against all ungodliness and unrighteousness of men.[5]

It is no use, as we have seen over and over again in the dogmatic annals of the Church, allowing the fear of unworthy conceptions and degrading superstitions to spoil and obliterate those delicate shades of doctrine, which offer themselves so easily to distortion, and yet which add not a little to the beauty and soundness of the conception.

[1] See Ellicott, "Salutary Doctrine," p. 79.
[2] Wordsworth, "The One Religion," p. 209.
[3] St. Anselm, "Cur Deus Homo," i. 23.
[4] St. John iii. 36.
[5] Rom. i. 18. See also "Christ in the World," p. 124, Foley, "Donnelan Lectures."

Holy Scripture exhibits, and it is unnecessary to pursue it further, through the New Testament, a consistent witness to an objective fact, which took place in the spiritual world, known as the Atonement, whereby the relations of God to man, and of man to God, were completely altered; whereby sin obtained a check, and the world and mankind were in some way readjusted.

When the Divine Liturgy, at the most solemn moment of its representation of Calvary, speaks of the "full, perfect, and sufficient sacrifice, oblation, and satisfaction" offered by Christ on the cross, we feel that it is only echoing the language of Holy Scripture, language to be justified by the long experience of humanity, and spiritual insight, rather than justified by argument, or defended on *a priori* grounds of the human sense of judicial fitness.

"The infinite worth of the Son of God"[1] is proved again and again in this struggling, sin-stricken life.

(2.) And the other great strain which loudly sounds its redemptive note is *grace*.

---

[1] Hooker, "Eccl. Pol.," v. 523.

Prayer runs with its golden thread of reconciliation right through the sacred record of God's dealings with man.

It would be a shallow estimate which saw no blessing to the worshipper accruing from the system of sacrifice in the Old Testament, however powerless in itself; but in the New Testament, running parallel with the Atonement, or rather coming out of it, we are struck with the intense prominence assigned to a system of grace.

The foundations of a Divine Kingdom, a precinct within which man has a direct access to God, seems as prominent as the offering of the sacrificial victim. The Church appears as no apostolic afterthought, but as a fully developed plan, formed in embryo by the Redeemer's hand, containing in itself its own power of development or realization. Sacraments appear, again, not as symbolic mementos to console those who had not listened to the actual voice of Jesus Christ, nor witnessed His power, but as stern necessities. "Except a man be born of water and of the Spirit, he cannot enter into the kingdom of God."[1] "Go ye therefore, and make disciples of all the nations, baptizing them into the name of the Father and of the Son and of the Holy Ghost."[2]

The converted Saul is baptized, as the means whereby to wash away his sins.[3] He answers the Philippian gaoler, who inquired about salvation, by inculcating the necessity of belief on the Lord Jesus Christ, and the first stage of that belief is indicated by submitting to baptism.[4] "The like figure whereunto even baptism doth also save us,"[5] is another apostolic expression familiar to us.

And no less, if we believe the universal testimony of the Church up to the sixteenth century, and refuse to be led away by the exigencies of controversy which caused, first, a Roman Cardinal, and then Protestant teachers to deny the applicability of the sixth chapter of St. John to the Holy Eucharist; if we follow the guidance of our Prayer-book, which is explicit[6] on this

---

[1] St. John iii. 5.   [2] St. Matt. xxviii. 19.
[3] Acts ix. 18.   [4] Acts xvi. 83.   [5] 1 St. Pet. iii. 21.
[6] See third exhortation in the service of Holy Communion, "Dearly beloved in the Lord."

point, we shall hear again our Blessed Lord speaking of the Sacrament of the Altar, not as a spiritual luxury, nor as a meditative elevation, but as a necessity of life. And so, when Christianity appears outside the pages of the Bible, and is noticed by non-Christian writers, or defended by apologists, the Holy Eucharist appears as the most prominent feature of its worship.

It is necessary to insist on this, because there is always a tendency to regard the Church as a human institution in which those who were animated by a common tradition crystallized and preserved their experience, instead of being, as it is, an integral part of the Divine plan; or to regard salvation through Christ, and salvation through the Sacraments, as being in some way opposed, instead of again being the same thing.

The fact being that Holy Scripture exhibits a system of salvation which may be symbolized by the parable of the Good Samaritan.

Mankind on his journey through the world is fallen upon by the thieves of sin, who strip him of his robe of original righteousness, wound him, and leave him half dead in "trespasses and sins." The patriarchal dispensation went by, without helping him, on the other side. The Levitical Law just looked at him—by the law is the knowledge of sin[1]—and passed by on the other side without conferring material help. Christ was moved with compassion, came down to him, bound up his wounds, pouring in the oil and wine—here we have the Atonement,—set him on His own merits, because he could not walk alone, and took him to His Church, where He left provision for his spiritual sustenance, with a promise of an abiding provision for his continuous support:—there is the whole system of grace or sanctification.

We, in our own efforts to help a man, recognize that we have only done half when we attempt to repair the past; a considerable, the main part of our endeavour lies before us, in providing against a recurrence of such calamities in the future.

Atonement and Sanctification, these are the two

[1] Rom. iii. 20.

streams into which Holy Scripture represents the redemptive force as gathered for the restoration of fallen man.

II.

Now the question remains, and it is a large one, with only a very short time in which to consider it: Are there, once more, traces of this in our experience?

(1.) There is a widespread feeling, and there is a certain justification for it, that we live in an age which makes little of the Atonement; that Evolution lands us in the Incarnation; and man is so pleased with his powers and his possibilities, and what he is going to make out of this world, that he neither feels the need of, nor stops to think much about the Atonement.

That there is a certain amount of truth in this, we cannot deny. There is nothing like the sense of sinfulness, and of the appalling power of sin, to throw a man on the sense of the need of an Atonement, the desire for help; "our readiness to believe in the Redeemer does, in fact, depend upon the strength of the impression made upon our minds by the sin of the world. Whatever impulse to belief may come from intellectual or æsthetic considerations, the primary force which stimulates to belief is the desire for righteousness and the sense of sin." [1]

So that with any weakening of the sense of sin, we may expect a corresponding weakening of the sense of the Atonement, as a necessary or even desirable fact.

However this may be, is there, in experience, any trace of a great fact, such as Holy Scripture represents the Atonement to have been? Can we say with Bishop Andrewes, boldly, "all the green things of the earth are better for the Incarnation"? Is there any sign of that which is dimly hinted at in the Epistle to the Ephesians: "That in the dispensation of the fulness of times He might gather together in one all things in Christ, both which are in heaven, and which are on earth; even in Him"? [2] or again: "And, having made peace

[1] Canon Gore, "Bampton Lectures," ii. 3, p. 37. [2] Eph. i. 10.

through the blood of His cross, by Him to reconcile all things unto Himself; by Him, I say, whether they be things in earth, or things in heaven"?[1] Is there any trace of that state of things, or answering to it, which pious souls looked forward to as "the consolation of Israel"?[2]

Is there a real progress in the good of the world, a progress only possible, because an incubus or dead-weight of sin has been taken away? Are the *Gesta Christi*—such as the abolition of slavery; the disgrace attached to, and the general giving up of wars of aggression; the emancipation of women; the greater care of the old, the infirm, children, lower animals;—are all these merely due to the working of Christian precepts, or something more?

The wonderful development of the world, in beauty, in resource, in function,—has there been an emancipation? has a huge tax been taken off —a bar—a hindrance?

This can only be a speculation, and it would be a waste of time to argue it. The Christian world

[1] Col. i. 20.   [2] St. Luke ii. 25.

is very different to the Pagan world, and a Christian country to a country where no Christian influence, or at the best an influence only diluted in civilization, has reached. But again, this may be *post hoc, non propter hoc*—subsequent, not consequent. Although for all that we may note it.

But here again we must betake ourselves to human experience.

Certainly the ideal of conduct has been raised.[1] Granted that this ideal is imperfectly realized, still it is there, and men and women are reaching out after it in a way in which they would not, if it were utterly impracticable.

But even more, in dealing with sin most of us are aware of the haunting nature of our sense of the past: the irretrievable character of a mistake, or a sin; the utter inadequacy of a mere healthy return to a higher line of conduct while the past remains; such as we see again and again portrayed in the deep sense of the ancient world, in Nemesis, in the Furies, in the impossibility of getting out of the shadow of the past guilt.

[1] Foley, "Donnellan Lectures," p. 111.

Does not human experience help us here? Does not the familiar figure of Christian laying down his bundle at the foot of the Cross represent a very real, and, thank God, a very common experience, whereby, through virtue of the Cross, and the love which streams from it, a man may get rid of the disabling sense of shame, of a moral disability, a leprosy which makes him unfit and unable to move? Sin can be removed, not only as clamouring for punishment in the shape of guilt, but as disabling the footsteps, in the sense of dishonour, so that a man can say, "I am not ashamed of what I was, being what I am."

Beyond the sense of an offence against God, and a cruel injury done to man, we are conscious of an eternal fitness of things, which, in some way, we have violated. There are absolute laws of right and wrong, as well as positive laws of God, which, if we transgress them, give us a sense of moral degradation, even if no eye sees us sin; and although God forgives us, right is right and wrong is wrong, in the sense that parallel straight lines can never meet, nor straight lines ever enclose a space.

And Christ can put us right even here. We can, if we accept Him, put ourselves once more in our true position, as we see in the familiar instance of penitence being accepted in our own minds almost as an equivalent for innocence. So that we may say that to apprehend the teaching of Christ, is to put ourselves almost right in the nature of things.

This realization of the Atonement, as of a thing once effected, must needs be shadowy and difficult of proof.

(2.) But our task becomes lighter when we pass on to consider Grace as the manifestation of the sanctifying results of the Atonement with which we are most familiar.

The two difficulties which the Fall brought with it, to our individual souls, we have already considered.

They were difficulties which lurked in two main directions—in heredity and in environment. And if we examine life in these two directions, we shall find the most characteristic examples of the working of Grace.

Now, however mysterious it may be, and whatever we may have to say to theories of traducianism, the question of heredity and of its extraordinary power for good or for evil, *i.e.*, to be quite plain, the transmission of good and bad qualities from parents and grandparents, and ancestors further back, to the children, is a fact which no one would care to deny; or, what is more mysterious still, the transmission of passing phases of character or disposition marking a peculiar stage in the parents' career,[1] a common example of which may be seen in one member of a family who, in disposition and in other ways, is different to all the rest.

It can easily be seen what a terrible power this incidence of heredity might exercise over a man. "Bad I was born, bad I am, bad I shall probably continue, bad I shall die," he might say, as has been said, in his despair. But now mark how exactly grace meets this initial difficulty, in Baptism.

It may be roughly asserted that man, without the aid of something to counteract an heredity, always bad to a certain extent in all of us, "as in

[1] Cook's Boston Lectures, "Love and Marriage," p. 148.

Adam all die," would be quite unable to be good, in the sense at all events required by Christianity.

I am not denying the immense natural virtues displayed by pre-Christian men and women, but it is not a little significant that one of the most noble exponents of ideal morality in the ancient world makes terms with sensual sin, as if it were hopeless to eradicate it.

Now Baptism recognizes heredity in the sense that, as an initial condition to a Christian life, a man must be reborn, and become a child of grace instead of a child of wrath. Then it might be supposed that the font produced a race of children uniformly levelled to a type of Christian excellence, which in subsequent life they might either develop or disperse in proportion as they worked or did not work together with grace. But this is not so. Look at the difference in Christian characters, and what is more, see how Holy Baptism has seized on the very inequalities of heredity and made them distinctive features in the Christian character.

You know how an architect will seize on the roughness and peculiarity of an uneven site, and make them features of beauty in his design. In like manner the Holy Spirit deals with the inequalities of heredity. Look at that noble resentment, which exercises a commanding power of discipline, which makes itself felt for good, in forming the character of the family, the household, the department of life in which the man works, which leaves its mark upon the very institutions of the country. That might have been, if unregenerated, a mere impotent, fruitless anger.

Look at that peaceful repose of mind again, which soothes and calms all with which it comes in contact, unruffled, undisturbed, itself a very embodiment of "the tranquillity of order." That, if left unregenerated, might have been sloth.

It is so, could we but trace it, with many other of the distinguishing marks in the saintly character —they are regenerated faults. And so with all our character; no Christian man who has been baptized, can plead heredity as too strong for him. All his faults, all his tendencies as well as all his virtues, have been passed through the font.

See how experience justifies the stress laid on

Holy Baptism as a necessity. It is the foundation excavated out of evil, on which alone Grace can build up its structure of virtue.

As with heredity, so with environment, man's other difficulty. We shall find grace ever ready to cope with the difficulties presented by life, and experience bearing testimony to the voice of Revelation which announces the institution and insists on the importance of such means.

In the short space that remains, I must pass by Absolution, which deals with actual sin, as Baptism deals with original sin, and not only procures forgiveness of sin, but forgiveness in a certain way, just as a skilful physician does not address himself to the immediate manifestation of the disease, but goes to the root, and, while he removes the disease, prevents, if possible, its recurrence.

And I would note particularly the much-misunderstood importance, in the place it occupies as the complement of Baptism—of Confirmation. Most unfortunately we have so long regarded Confirmation as the conscious renewal of baptismal vows (which, as a matter of fact, does not belong to it essentially at all), that we have forgotten that aspect of this means of grace, which exhibits it as the divine indwelling of the Holy Ghost in the temple reared up for it in Baptism, as the consecration of the temple which Baptism has built, which strengthens a man against the evil which is always ready to spring upon him from his environment, which, in fact, seeks help and perfection, not from an environment made harmless, by good food, good drains, good houses, good education, culture, refinement of all sorts, but by a braced, strengthened, sanctified will. It is often the case that Confirmation is the turning-point in a person's career, not because then he has scientifically apprehended his enemies, and knows how to meet them, but because the strength of grace has got the better of the force of evil habit; and when the devil springs out of environment, he at least does not find the house empty, and so we are led to that most blessed of all the means of grace, where, to the devout soul, his own self becomes fulfilled with Christ, in a life where the Christian can say, by virtue of the presence of Christ coming through the Sacrament of the Altar; "Not I, but Christ liveth in me."

The experience which we have now gone through is one which most of us can confirm out of our own individual histories.

It is thus that we are able to read so constantly, and meditate with such profit on God's Holy Word. It is not a dead record, nor the sound of one who has a pleasant voice and can play well on an instrument.[1] It is the record of the struggles and sorrows of our own individual lives. It is the hope and earnest of our ultimate victory.

[1] Ezek. xxxiii. 32.

INDEX

A

Abraham, testimony of his life to the value of prayer, 21

Absolution procures remission of actual sin, 190

Abstinence, a necessity to the spiritual man, 59

Adam, his living soul, the result of a special act of creation, not a mere process of evolution, 29; signs of his original perfection still evident, 40; inherited weakness of man, the price of his fall, 48; the origin of sin traced by Holy Scripture to his fall, 27, 96

Affection, its proper place in the well-ordered life, 45

Agnosticism more prevalent than atheism in the present day, 3, 5

Alexander, 26

Almsgiving, positive duty of, to the Christian, 89

"Analogy," Bishop Butler's, 10

Ananias and Sapphira, an example of Satan's skilful method of attack, 107

Andrewes, Bishop, his estimate of the results of the Incarnation, 182

Anger, in the regenerated man, becomes noble resentment, 189

Anselm, St., 77 n., 175 n.

Appetite must be made obedient to the will, 156

Aristotle, 81, 96

Atheism, in the seventeenth century practical rather than scientific, 3; of the present day, 3, 4; of a life of material gratification, 5

Atonement, the, a great fact in the scheme of Redemption, 149, 171; the important position assigned to it in Holy Scripture, 171, 172, 175, 176; made by Christ as the representative of the human race, 173, 174; thought little of by some people at the present day, 181; the sense of its need, deepened by the sense of sin, 181, 182; rids a man of the sense of moral disability, 185

Augustine, St., 77 n., 164

Avarice, a corruption of thrift, 142

B

Baptism, lays the foundation of Christian virtues, 41, 190; meets the difficulty of heredity, 188; produces Christian virtues out of the inequalities of heredity, 188; finds its complement in Confirmation, 190

Baring-Gould, 166 n.

Bible, the, its simplicity ridiculed by Satan, 118; reveals the severe consequences which follow sin, 121, 122; deals principally with the history of the Fall and the Redemption, 75

Body, the, the third and lowest part of man's nature, 39; is not meant by God to be suppressed, 163; has been for ever dignified by the Incarnation, 72

Boyle, Robt., the will of, 1

Buddhism, the inadequate sense of sin in the religion of, 79

Buddhist, the prayer-wheel of, 22

Butler's, Bishop, analogy, 10, 27 n.

C

Calvary, the only adequate measure of sin, 126

Character, Christian, developed by suffering, 71; assisted in its formation by the will, 161; the power of redemptive love exhibited by its beauty, 166; not dependent upon environment, 166, 167; consists of more than the exhibition of natural virtues, 167-170; developed by grace out of the inequalities of heredity, 189; many of its marks are regenerated faults, 189

Charles IX. of France, incident in the life of, 138

Christian evidences, in themselves unsatisfying, 4

Christian, the, the idea of spiritual eating and drinking familiar to a, 32; the spirit, the guiding power of his life, 38; accused of inventing sin for the purpose of remedying it, 74; shamed by his incapacity for spiritual exercises, 89; should endeavour to neutralize the effect of sin in his own life, 94; must bring his whole being under the obedience of Christ, 163

Christianity, its reality and importance, 7; affords us an explanation of life, 8; necessarily appeals to the spiritual, rather than the rational side of nature, 25; Satan tries to relax its strictness, 118; turns the world's curses into blessings, 152; its effects upon the world, 182-184

Church, Dean, 19

Church, the, and State, condition of, in the seventeenth century, 1, 2; modern indifference to its claims and obligations, 6; unaffected by the doctrine of evolution, 30; its special work is to counteract the effects of the Fall, 41; its proper attitude in regard to social reform, 60-73; objections urged against its doctrine of eternal punishment, 124-126; endued with sacramental Grace, 163; privilege of being in the Church useless without effort, 165; the importance of the delicate shades in its doctrine, 175; is the means of access to God, 177; founded by Christ Himself, and endowed with sacramental life, 177, 180

Civilization does not of itself conduce to moral development, 151

Confirmation, its importance as the complement of Baptism, 191

Conscience viewed as identical with the spirit, 38

Cook, "Boston Lecture," 129, 130 n., 187 n.

Creation, the whole of it implicated in the Fall, 32; branded with failure, 55; may yet be redeemed from Satan's power, 73

Cross, the, the only adequate measure of sin, 96, 126; led up to by the ancient system of sacrifices, 173; the power by which man can alone rid himself of the disabling sense of sin, 185

Crucifix, the, the underlying idea of, 20

Cynicism, its evil effect on spiritual life, 113

D

Darwin, p. 28 n.
David, his penitence does not do away with his punishment, 130
Degeneration, the natural tendency of man in consequence of the Fall, 42, 46
Deism, largely prevalent in the seventeenth century, 2, 3

Delitzsch, Commentary of, on Genesis, 31
Demon worship, its development and results in African systems, 105; a society said to be established in Paris for that purpose, 105
Depression, its source to be traced to the Devil, 117
Despair of the ancient world, a witness to a deep sense of sin, 80, 81
Devil, the, Holy Scripture attributes temptation to him, 99; belief in his personality objected to, 99, 100; his personality clearly defined in Holy Scripture, 101; the consummate skill of his attacks, 106; the appropriateness and meaning of the term, described, 112–117, 155
"Dies Iræ," 19
Diggle, J. W., 4 n.
Dogmatic Faith, a witness to the weakness of unassisted human nature, 92, 93
Drummond, 41 n.

E

Ellicott, Bishop, 52 n., 172 n., 175 n.
Environment, man's, included in the evil consequences of the Fall, 34, 53, 57; in itself, detrimental to his spiritual life, 58–60, 69, 151; can only be improved by improving man, 152; the triumph of Grace over it, 153; mistakes made in artificially creating it, 163; its difficulties met by sacramental Grace, 190

Epicurean, the, his attitude in regard to pain, 69
Esther, Queen, by her intervention, saved the Jews and shadowed forth the work of Christ, 151
Everlasting, term used by our Blessed Lord to convey a sense of permanency, 132, 133
Evil, its origin a puzzle to humanity, 27; traced by Holy Scripture to the Fall, 27; strong bias towards it in man, 37; costs us nothing to commit, 42; external knowledge of evil, different to interior sympathetic knowledge of it, 48; a sense of evil may exist in man without the sense of sin, 76; attributed by Holy Scripture to a personal agent, 99, 103; its presence in the world perplexing to man, 128-130; causes depression in the spiritual life, 142; re-adapted by grace to great uses, 153; certain of its phenomena only known to the spiritual man, 120
Evil One, the, significant titles of, in Holy Scripture, 111; accurately described in the word Devil, 114; described, by our Blessed Lord, as a murderer, 119; belief in his personality confirmed by our Blessed Lord, 101-103
Evil suggestions, the Devil's first plan of attack, 107
Evolution, popularity of the doctrine of, 28; Christian faith untouched by it, 29; must not too confidently be assumed to explain all existing phenomena, 30, 50; anterior to the Bible narrative of the Fall, 31
Excavator, the spade of the, a new factor in the science of historical criticism, 8; confirms tradition regarded as mythical and legendary, 9; the same plan to be adopted in searching human experience, 10, 13

F

Failure, in humanity, the result of the Fall, 37; branded on the face of creation, 53, 55; a missing of purpose, 56; the experience of the saints in their struggle against sin, 86
Faith, a mark of Christian character, 169; the dogmatic, is a witness to human weakness, 92
Fall, the, represented by Holy Scripture as accounting for evil, 27, 28; is an unpopular subject, 28, 31; remains untouched by the theory of evolution, 29; is not a simple fairy story, 32; there are real difficulties in connection with it, 33; a complete catastrophe according to the Bible, 33, 34; corroborated by human experience, 36; man's capacity for degradation one of its marks, 46; its effects on nationalities similar to that on individuals, 49; any scheme of evolution must make way for it, 50; its consequences on the world, 52; the cause of physical pain in man, 69; asserted by Holy Scripture to have been the action of

the Devil, 101; its consequences reversed by Redemption, 157

Fasting, its necessity in an unhealthy world, 59; the Christian's difficulty in practising it, 89

Fatalism produced by false views of temptation, 108

Flesh, the, an active ally of the Devil, 99

Flint, Professor, 41 n.

Foley's "Donnellan Lectures," 151, 175 n., 184 n.

Food, its mystery, in relation to character and habits, 32; the spiritual man has to guard against its dangers, 59

Francis, St., of Assisi, exhibits in his life that sense of sin found most prominently in saintly lives, 83; his reception of the sacred Stigmata, 134

Freewill respected by God, 143

G

Genesis corroborated by an appeal to the history of man, 36, 37

Gentleness, a mark of the Christian character, 169

Gluttony, 47, 142

God, tendency of the present day to live without God, 6, 11, 14; approached in three ways, worship, penitence, and prayer, 15, 23; worship reserved for God, 16, 18; sense of His presence means the sense of sin, 19, 20; speaks to the spiritual man through prayer and sacraments, 21, 22; deliberate worship of the noblest lives, a testimony that there is a personal God, 18; not to be falsely accused as to His purpose for man, 48; His love for the perfection of mankind, 49; the world's environment makes it difficult to read His will, 58; the world's development needs the sanctification of God, 73; a sense of alienation from, in the religions of the world, 79; personal love for Him, a thing to be aimed at, 95; significance of His names in Holy Scripture, 111; His relations with man broken by sin, 121; His wrath against sin, 122, 123; punishment for sin asserted to be contrary to His nature, 124; His action in allowing evil to exist in the world, a mystery to man, 128, 129; effects by Redemption the eternal purposes for which He created the world, 146; does not force man's will to act rightly, 162; man's difficulty in co-operating with Him, 165; is not to be blamed for our weakness, 165; reconciled to man through the Atonement, 174, 175

Good, only makes its way by an effort, 42; its difficulty of accomplishment experienced by the saints, 85, 91; its difficulty explained by Revelation as owing to the personal agency of the devil, 118; developed by redemptive power in the world, 148; the universality of the wish to be good a witness to redemptive power in the world, 154

Goodness, a mark of the Christian character, 169
Gore, Canon, 13 n., 24, 43 n., 77 n., 102, 108 n., 154 n., 182 n.
Grace, its important position in theology, 12; its power over evil, 153; sanctification effected by it, 163, 176; acts upon man through the Church, 164; conveys the benefits of the Atonement to man, 171, 186; the prominence assigned to it in the New Testament, 177; its power seen most characteristically in meeting the difficulties of heredity and environment, 187-192

H

Happiness, craving for, may be a bad sign, 116
Heard, 38 n.
Hebrew prophets, their denunciation of the world's degradation, 49; deepened man's sense of sin, 76, 96; their position as regards "the Law," 148
Herbert, George, 21 n.
Heredity, its poisonous entail, 48; man cursed in his, 52; a difficulty to thoughtful men, 129; is an undeniable fact, 187
Holland, Canon H. Scott, 4 n., 56 n.
Holy Scripture traces the origin of evil to the Fall, 27; does not infer that God only intended man to enjoy a maimed life, 48; its estimate of previous worlds, 53; describes the world as unhealthy, 54; sin inseparably bound up with its teaching, 75; the danger of misunderstanding its meaning, 92, 93; never varies in tracing evil suggestions to the devil, 99; cannot be used to oppose the doctrine of the personality of the devil, 103; significance of names and titles in, 111, 112; the revelation of God's wrath on sin in, 121, 123; exhibits the working out of the curse on sin, 123; objections to its doctrine of punishment on sin, 124, 125; represents punishment on sin as tremendous, 126; exhibits redemptive power in the world, 146, 153; the prominent position it assigns to the Atonement, 171, 175, 176; exhibits to us God's plan of salvation, in the Parable of the Good Samaritan, 179, 180
Holy Spirit finds His dwelling-place in the spirit of man, 38; the fruits of the Spirit, 168-170
Hooker, 176 n.
Hope, its redemptive power, 155
Human actions controlled by God, 14
Human experience corroborates the statements of Revelation that there is a personal God, 16; sin can be largely traced in, 78, 82; its testimony to the accusing nature of the devil, 119; its testimony in regard to sin and punishment, 127, 133; reveals redemptive power in the world, 134; points to Christian character as a proof of redemptive power, 166; traces of the

INDEX. 199

power of Atonement and grace in, 181, 182; exhibits a higher ideal of conduct through the power of grace, 184, 185

Human language, the difficulty of being good expressed in, 42; traces of sin in, 78, 82; incapable of expressing the mystery of the Atonement, 127

Human life, what it says of Revelation, 8; contains no common land outside restraint, 86; how affected by remorse, 136

Human nature said by Revelation to be bad, where it was once good, 11; traces of the Fall in, examined, 35, 47; composed of three parts — spirit, soul, and body, 38, 40; it is so bad that man must be born again, 41; shows traces of a great disorder, 43, 48; its sense of misery without God, 43; shows a startling confirmation of the narrative of the Fall, 51; its efforts to get rid of the sense of sin by sacrifice, 78; its powerlessness to eradicate evil, 86; if unassisted, is overmatched in the struggle with sin, 91; its traces of redemptive power examined, 150, 170; mistaken views as to its depravity and capacity for goodness, 87; "the desire to be good" exhibits redemptive power at work, 154; placed by Jesus Christ under the influence of grace, 163

Human race made reparation in Christ on the Cross, 173

Human religions show traces of sin, 78, 80

Humanity, the origin of evil a difficult question to, 27; the world can only be developed by a humanity alive with Christ, 72; the phenomenon of "possession" as bearing on, 104

Hutchings, 101 n.

I

Illingworth, 25 n., 89 n., 137 n., 139 n., 161
Imagination, 36, 39, 45
"Imitation of Christ," 71 n.
Incarnation, the, honour conferred on man by the, 36; the body for ever dignified by the, 72; part of the scheme of Redemption, 149; Christ by the Incarnation represented the whole human race, 173
Indian philosophy, the wail of, 81
Indolence develops into sloth, 142
Innocency, its value unrealized until it is gone, 139
Irritability may develop into the deadly sin of anger, 142
Islam, a very slight apparent sense of sin in, 79
Ixion, the punishment of, 133

J

Jesus Christ, His attitude towards physical pain, 69, 71; sin bruised and beaten down in His person, 76; His power necessary for the realization of spiritual ideals, 88; the emphasis He lays on diabolic agency, 103; places man in a consecrated precinct of Grace, 164; the whole human race made reparation to God in Him, 173; He alone could represent the world as it ought to be in the eyes of God, 174; reconciles man to God by His suffering, 174

Joy, a mark of the Christian character, 168

Judas, an example of Satan's skill in tempting, 107; an example of everlasting punishment, 122; falls in spite of his environment, 153

Justification, the perversion of the doctrine of, 87; the true explanation of, 87, 88

Juvenal, 49, 81

K

Keble, Mr., 19, 158
Kenosis, the Divine, cannot be reserved for selected cases, 103

L

Lacordaire, Père, 26 n., 43 n., 135
Latitudinarianism, 2
Law, of cause and effect passed upon the world, 152; transgression of, causes a sense of moral degradation, 185
Law, the. *See* Mosaic
Liddon, Dr., 12 n., 16 n., 19 n., 29 n., 74 n., 77 n., 82 n., 84 n., 94, 95 n.

Life, the melancholy and failure which brood over life point to the Fall, 37; its plans and modes affected by environment, 57; the influence of the world over, 58, 59; limited by death and conditioned by the Fall, 60; the devil's opposition to, 117; seems spent in repairs, instead of progress, 141; must be regulated by the will, 162; bears witness to the Redemptive power, 170

Liturgy, Divine, echoes Holy Scripture in speaking of Christ's sacrifice, 176

Longsuffering, part of the Christian character, 169

Lord, our Blessed, His dealing with social questions, 62; His choice of poverty, 63; refused to be eased of pain, 71; supports belief in the personality of the evil one, 101, 102; temptation to Him purely external, 109; defines the devil as a murderer, 119; His dealing with the question of everlasting punishment, 123, 133; intended to convey by His words the deadly nature of sin, 124, 131; derives virtues out of temptation, 153; speaks of the Eucharist as a necessity, 179

Love, the giving out of self to God and man, 168

Lower animals, the mystery of our relation to the, 32

Luciferans, a new society of devil-worshippers, said to have been started in Paris, 105

INDEX.

M

Man, represented by revelation as controlled by God, 11, 14; traces of religious experience to be found principally in the spiritual man, 13; has approached God in three ways, worship, penitence, and prayer, 15-23; the theory as to his origin, given by evolution, antecedent to the Fall, 28, 29; his complex nature, 36; has an evil bias, 37, 41; composed of spirit, soul, and body, 38-40; must be born again, 41; needs constant draughts of life in the Sacraments, 41; his nature thoroughly miserable without God, 43; his capacity for degradation, 46; his knowledge of sin intended by God to be external, 48; his history dealt with in the Bible, 51; involved in his downfall all creation, 54; his desire in life for the most part the accumulation of material wealth, 61, 65; is more important than his environment, 68, 52; baffled by the mystery of pain, 69; progress in the world must first begin in man, 72; his sense of sin gradually deepened, 75, 76; his degradation expressed in ancient writings, 80, 81; his struggle against sin, 85, 91; his inability to be just with God, 97; the training of his intellect does not qualify him for spiritual experience, 120; his relations with God broken by sin, 121; can commit sin, but cannot undo it, 127; his ideas of what the world ought to be contradicted by fact, 128-131; has to suffer the consequences of all mistakes, 130; suffers loss apart from God, 140; his whole life shaped by the promise of Redemption, 147; divine restlessness in man, 155-157; has to regulate his life by the use of his will, 162; draws support from the environment of Grace, 164; redeemed by Jesus Christ, becomes like God, 169; shares in the sufferings of Jesus Christ, 174; is reconciled to God through Jesus Christ, 174; his ideal raised by the Atonement, 184; can get rid of his sin by virtue of the Cross, 185; requires the aid of Grace to counteract his heredity and environment, 188

Materialism, 74

Material wealth, the main desire of man to accumulate, 61, 65

Matthew, St., rises to the apostleship in spite of his environment, 153

Max Müller, 18 n., 82 n.

Meditation, means of communion between the soul and God, 95

Meekness, a mark of the Christian character, 169

Melancholy, 37, 117

Memory, 36, 39, 45

Milligan, 125 n.

Mosaic Law, man's latent knowledge of sin deepened by, 75-96; developed the moral life of man, 148; and the prophets, 148

2 D

Moore, Aubrey, 28 n., 63 n.
Moslem, the, an example of the power of earnest prayer, 22

N

Nations, the consequences of the Fall apparent in the great life of, 49
Natural religion, 3
Natural selection, 34, 54
Nature. *See* Human nature
Nemesis, its prominence in the Greek tragedies, 133
Nero, 46

P

Paget, Sir James, 161 n.
Pain, physical, a survival of the Fall, 69; Jesus Christ's attitude towards it, 69-71; the Christian use of, 152
Passions, 45
Paul, St., his account of the Fall and its consequences on creation, 53; his spirit of immolation, 135; inculcates the necessity of Sacraments, 178
Peace, that which pervades the heart of the Christian, 168
Penitence, one of the three roads leading to God, 15-23; can never take the place of innocence, 139
Personality, 36; man's unique, 36; careful investigation of one's own personality shows traces of the Fall, 50
Philosophy, 14, 31
Poets, Greek and Latin, on punishment of sin, 133

Poor, the, 64
"Possession," 104, 106
Poverty inculcated by our Blessed Lord, 63
Prayer, one of the three paths which lead to God, 16, 21, 22, 23, 95; the Christian shamed by his incapacity for, 89; Satan puts difficulties in the way of, 118; runs right through the records of God's dealing with man, 177
Prayer-book, explicit testimony to the Catholic interpretation of St. John vi., 178
Predestination, 36
Privilege useless without effort, 165
Punishment for sin, as dealt with in the New Testament, 121; spoken of by our Blessed Lord as a warning to man, 124; indignantly denied by many as contrary to God's love and mercy, 124; attempt to mitigate the doctrine (1) by the universalists, 125; (2) by those who contend that sin and its punishment will be finally eradicated, 125; (3) by those who point to the extermination of the sinner, 126; is best measured by the mystery of the Atonement, 127; future punishment no greater difficulty than present, 128; its justice a difficulty to thoughtful men, 130; its characteristics—permanence, 132-136, 144; severity, 136-139, 144; loss, 138-144; its permanence portrayed in the Greek and Latin poets, 133; remembrance of past sin a punish-

ment to holy men, 135, 143, 144
Pusey, Dr., his sense of sin, 19, 84

R

Reason, 36, 45, 57
Redemption, revelation exhibits a well-ordered scheme of, 75, 146–149; achieved by the Atonement, 149-171; extended to man by means of the Sacraments, 149; takes place in spite of, by means of the world, 150, 153; its power seen at work in the saintly life, 157; reverses the effects of the Fall, 157; strengthens man's will, 159, 162; by the power of Grace, enables him to rise from the dust, 164, 170; revealed in the refinements of the Christian character, 168; witnessed to by the phenomena of life, 170; finds its most intense expression in the Atonement and the power of grace, 171
Religion, 5, 15, 58; God knows nothing of mechanical, 165
Religious experience will be found in the spiritual man, 13
Remorse, 115; its darkness on human life, 137; may be turned to good or bad account, 137, 138
Repentance hindered by Satan, 118
Resentment, noble, regenerated anger, 189
Resolutions, 45; broken — no sign of failure, 115
Respect, 45
Restlessness, Divine—in man, a sign of Redemption, 155, 157

Revealed religion just as important now as ever, 7; the traces of sin which run through it, 78
Revealed truth, 23
Revelation, Christian, felt to be antiquated in many quarters, 5, 6; confirmed by excavations in human experience, 10; has a great deal to say about God, 11; interpenetrated with the phenomena of sin, 12, 74; its testimony regarding the world, 52; is its representation of sin true? 85; exhibits a well-ordered scheme of Redemption, 145, 147–149
Riches, 61, 64, 67
Rivalry develops into envy, 142
Romanes, 24 n., 43 n., 102, 103 n., 139 n., 140 n.
Ruskin, Professor, 55 n.

S

Sabatier, M., on the life of St. Francis, 84, 134
Sacraments, modern indifference to, 6; means of communion with God, 21, 95; Baptism necessary for man, 41; danger of misunderstanding grace of, 92, 93; preparation for them hindered by Satan, 118; apparently existing side by side with sin in man, 165; seen in the New Testament to be a stern necessity, 177; St. John vi. must be taken to refer to the Holy Eucharist, 178; not opposed to Christ, 179; Holy Eucharist most blessed means of grace, 191
Sacrifice, of the Altar, 18; the

most obvious expression of sin in the religions of the world, 78; position assigned to it in Holy Scripture, 172, 173; ancient sacrifices powerless for the remission of sins, 173; reconciled God and man, 174; the "full, perfect, and complete," 176

Saints, the deepest sense of sin found in their lives, 83; tell us of their failure to reach an ideal, 85; tell us of a sense of injury done to a personal God, 89; their love of austerities, 134, 135; their sense of the need of atonement, 135; desire for goodness developed in them, 156

Salisbury, Lord, 29 n., 30 n., 54 n.

Salvation, St. Paul urges the necessity of sacraments for salvation, 178; symbolized by the parable of the Good Samaritan, 179

Sarcasm, its evil power on spiritual life, 113

Satan, the means by which he tempted man at the Fall, 32; temptation attributed by Holy Scripture to him, 99; *his personality* emphasized in Holy Scripture, 101; emphasized by our Lord, 101-103; the testimony of history to his presence, 104; the testimony of spiritual men, 109; the word expresses his character, 117; opposes all attempts to live a Christian life, 118; described by our Lord as a murderer, 119

Saul, his temptation, 101; his punishment, 130

Saul. *See* St. Paul.

Sayce, A. H., 9 n.

Schultz, 112 n.

Science, 21, 36

Scruples suggested to man by the devil, 116

Self-interest, 45

Sentiment, 39

Sensualist, 47

Sin, the whole of Revelation, interpenetrated with the phenomena of sin, 12; the sense of sin—in the savage, 18; the sense of sin becomes acute in the spiritual man, 18, 83, 96; a sense of God's presence produces a sense of sin, 19; a powerful influence which has shaped and directed the course of religion from the first, 74; inseparably bound up with Scripture teaching, 75, 76; a sense of evil may exist without a sense of sin, 76; the definition and history of, 77; finds its most striking expression in the religions of the world by sacrifice, 78, 96; expressed in the writings of the best minds, 80, 81, 96; expressed in human language, 82, 96; the struggle to conquer it, after it has been detected, 85, 86, 91; its power and universality, 88, 94; neglect of precaution against it, 91; is a great mistake, 93; is a catastrophe, 93; is a great loss, 94, 139, 140, 141, 142; cannot exist beneath the arms of the Cross, 95; will always be an annoyance, 96; temptation ripens into sin, over the prostrate will, 107; revelation of God's wrath in Holy Scripture against, 121; much

INDEX.

greater than its apparent importance, 121, 126; its deadly nature emphasized by Our Blessed Lord, 124; man can bring it on but not take it off, 127; a mystery which may be seen, but cannot be explained, 131; its cruel effects on men's lives, 136; its power to torture the pure heart, 138; deprives man of priceless blessings, 139; the seven deadly sins and their dangers, 142; checked by the Atonement, 176; a sense of the want of Atonement comes from a sense of sin, 181; sense of sin, primary impulse to belief, 182; disabling sense of sin removed by virtue of the Cross, 185

Sloth, 189

Social questions, the position of the Church in regard to, 60, 69; humanity alive with Christ can alone develop the world, 72

Sophocles, sense of sin expressed in his writings, 80

Soul, second part of man's incorporeal nature, 39; its maimed activities, 44; becomes aware of sin first, by a sense of loss, 142; cannot be satisfied by the appetite, 156

Spirit, the, the organ of God—consciousness in man, 38; the guiding power of a Christian's life, 38; void and unused in many people, 43; a ruin in some cases, 44

Spiritual experience, where loss arising from sin is most felt, 141

Spiritual disease, atrophy a common form of, 155

Spiritual man, the, his testimony to the statement of Revelation that there is a personal God, 14; impelled to reverence a being outside him, 16; in whom the sense of sin becomes most acute, 18, 83, 94; does not discard prayer, 21; conscious of the world's environment, 58; cannot let himself go, 59; sin almost too much for him, 91; proclaims the utter inability to be just with God, 97; the fact of his being tempted, a proof of the personality of Satan, 109; temptation becomes more external as he approaches Christ, 110; finds the titles of the Evil One appropriate, 112, 118; best qualified to judge as to the source of temptation, 119, 120; the unhappiness which come upon him, on the committal of sin, 137

Spiritualism, 105

Spirituality, 17

Stoic, the, attitude towards pain, 69

Subjective argument, objections to this line of argument answered, 23

T

Tacitus, 49, 81

Tantalus, 138

Taylor, Jeremy, 11, 79 n.

Temperance, power of using the things of this life rightly, 169

Temptation closely connected with the Fall, 98; attributed by Holy Scripture to Satan,

99, 104; unalterable plan of attack, 106; ripens into sin when the will consents, 107; its authorship an important question, 107, 108; of good men, points to a personal agent, 109; skilfully manipulated and marvellously adjusted, 110; can be understood properly by spiritual men only, 120; the virtues derived from, 152

Tertullian, 11, 79 n.

Theology, the important position it assigns to Grace, 12

Thucydides, 81

U

Universalists, their objection to the doctrine of eternal punishment, 125

V

Victory over sin won by hope, 155; over the appetites, produces strength of character, 156

Virgil, 133

Virtue, the strength implied in the term, 42; reproaches us when we commit sin, 138; in pre-Christian men and women, 188

W

Westcott, Bishop, 68

Will, the, 45, 57; attacked by the Evil One, 106; consent of the will necessary before temptation ripens into sin; 107; can be strengthened by Redemptive love or degraded to the service of the passions, 159; its sovereignty over man's actions, 160, 162; must regulate a man's life, 162; the object of Redemptive power is to strengthen it, 162; its freedom respected by God, 163; everything (including Grace) must be accepted by it, 165

Wordsworth, Bishop, 48, 49 n., 78, 79 n., 173 n., 175 n.

World, the, 11, 17, 21, 52; the failure which passed over it, 54; rightly indicated by Holy Scripture as unhealthy, 56, 59, 63; its influence over mankind in history and religion, 58; that taint which is renounced at the Font, 60; is not so incurably bad that it is not worth thinking about, 72; may be rescued from the clutches of Satan, 73; powerful ally of Satan, 99; is not what man would have expected it to be, 128-130; presents difficulties equally difficult to solve as those of a future life, 143; Redemption working in it, 146; Redemption by means of it, 150; law of cause and effect passed upon it, 152; its unsatisfying nature to the saints of God, 156

Worship, instinctive, of God, 15; the expression of homage reserved for God, 16; of the noblest lives is a testimony that there is a personal God, 18

PRINTED BY WILLIAM CLOWES AND SONS, LIMITED,
LONDON AND BECCLES.

www.ingramcontent.com/pod-product-compliance
Lightning Source LLC
Chambersburg PA
CBHW021840230426
43669CB00008B/1027